through the
SANDS of TIME

Past **Life Dramas** *Present* **Life Lessons**

By

Saundra Cindy Blum

Copyright © 2012 Saundra Cindy Blum
All Rights Reserved

ISBN: 1484114612
ISBN 13: 9781484114612

Library of Congress Control Number: 2013907696
CreateSpace Independent Publishing Platform
North Charleston, South Carolina

Table of Contents

Acknowledgments — v

Introduction — vii
    Overview — vii
    The Predicates of Past Life Regression — viii
    Format of a Typical Therapy Session — ix
    My Journey into Past-Life Work — xiii

Chapter One	Relationships and Soul Mates	1
Chapter Two	Physical Illness and Maladies	31
Chapter Three	Unworthiness	57
Chapter Four	Fears and Phobias	77
Chapter Five	Children	99
Chapter Six	Weight Issues	117
Chapter Seven	Victimization	143
Chapter Eight	Patterns	165
Chapter Nine	Addictions	189
Chapter Ten	Glossary and Capabilities	211

Messages from Spirit — 237

About the Author — 243

ACKNOWLEDGMENTS

This book has been a reflective journey for me. Although I only started to write it a couple of years ago, the format and stories have come from over the last twenty-five years.

I have to first start thanking my clients for the beautiful and not-so-beautiful stories, channelings, and lessons they have taught me. They have been my greatest teachers.
I sit humble and in gratitude.

I would next like to thank all of those who put time into typing, editing, and reading my book. Thank you, Jessica, Shira, Patricia, and Pete, for your timeless help. When I could read or edit no more, you were all there to carry on.

Thank you, Robyn and Joe, for reading my book and writing a beautiful endorsement for the book, and my dear friend Rachael, who is a photo genius. I am blessed to have such inspirational and insightful people understanding and acknowledging the value of this work.

I finally thank my loving and supportive husband, Michael, without whom I would not have been able to do my work or write this book. I also thank my children, Briana, Jordan, and Rachael, who were strong enough to have a mother who worked out of the box and who flourished in their unconditional love.

I would also like to thank my sister Nancy, who has been a great support and who has shared countless conversations about spirituality with me.

DEDICATION

This book is dedicated to my mom and sister Ricki, who were my greatest cheerleaders yet who were unsure that we do live on. Since their passing, they have communicated with me and told me I was right: we don't die, and we will be back together in our future lives.

Introduction

Overview

There is a tremendous shift in our consciousness on this planet. We are a nation of seekers, yearning to understand more and more of who we are and what our purpose is. Many of us have undergone one or more forms of psychological therapy to solve life's problems and find answers to our probing and sometimes life-long questions. Yet most of us feel something is still missing, and there are many answers we are desperately seeking.

Why do we seem to repeat patterns in relationships and other areas of our lives? Why do we have such unworthy feelings or suffer from chronic depression? Why did we need to endure the loss of a child or have to suffer from an abusive husband?

It is my belief, shared by others, that we will choose a life script before we come into this life, in our spiritual body, void of emotions, that will create a journey sometimes filled with trauma or difficult obstacles to push us into changing or learning our lesson. We would never choose these traumas or scripts in our physical and emotional bodies that we inhabit in this life, but on the spirit side we know what we need to karmically go through due to our past lives, and the people we need to go through it with, to grow and evolve. There is no judgment around the script; it is only there for our lessons. It is not only traumas and negativity that helps us grow but the one core lesson of love and forgiveness for self and others.

Footsteps Through the Sands of Time: Past-Life Dramas—Present-Life Lessons is the first book to offer answers to these questions through a compelling compilation of stories based on individual and factually verified regressions. Unlike other past-life books, Footsteps Through the Sands of Time: Past-Life Dramas—Present-Life Lessons breaks through the veil of secrecy by sharing the clients' most personal histories and intentions and is formatted like a private session with the therapist. Each story is centered on one session, covering a theme common and relatable to anyone. While the names of the clients and certain data have been changed, readers will get to see a rare and intimate view of a therapist's outline and interaction with the clients' regression from beginning to end. Culled from a database of more than four thousand clients, each story offers truth, insight, and enlightenment. The puzzle pieces these clients have discovered answer burning questions about their present-life dramas, questions the readers will identify with, seeing themselves in these stories and benefiting from the awareness, understanding, and connection the core lessons reveal.

The Predicates of Past Life Regression

The basis of Past Life Regression is a belief in the immortality of the soul. The second predicate is that souls are reborn and return to this world in order to learn, grow, and develop. As the soul is immortal, there is one individual soul that exists beyond a particular form or body and beyond a limited time. There are variations on the theme, of course, reflective of an individual's belief system, but these are the fundamental assumptions involved.

Individuals in this present life can access their previous lives. Being just part of a continuum, the soul in this life can tap into the full spectrum of experience that soul has undergone.

Format of a Typical Therapy Session

Identifying Issue

When a client settles in for a session with the therapist, the two review the issue that brings the client to the therapist's office. What is the fire underway in the client's life? What is the challenge or drama plaguing the client right now?

Then, with the issue fully identified, the two carefully formulate the intention for the session. This is the articulation of what they want discovered or healed. And it is the intention that is offered to the subconscious. Since the subconscious is literal, it is crucial to give the subconscious a precise intention so that it will retrieve the memory that will answer the question accurately and specifically.

For example, if the client currently has an abusive husband (the issue), the intention of the session might be to see why she chose an abusive husband in this life. Where are the roots of this problem, this issue? So the therapist would articulate the intention to be offered to the subconscious as: *look for the memory of the lifetime that brought her to experience an abusive husband in this life*.

Exploring the Past Life

As the client goes under a light hypnosis to access the past-life memory, the story begins to unfold. The therapist guides the client back to the childhood of the individual that emerges out of the past and then leads the client to review that past individual's life in five-year increments until that individual's death.

At that point, we learn how the client died, who was with him or her at the time of death, and, most importantly, we learn their all-important last thoughts. These last thoughts are often the foundation elements in their next incarnation (the client's current life), whether in the creation of a whole new life-drama or as some physical manifestation.

The therapist then helps the client review the past life uncovered by this process and answer the question: *If you could have changed anything, what would you have done differently?*

The client's answer to this question provides critical information that contributes to the life script of their subsequent incarnation—the client's current life.

Gaining Enlightenment

Once the therapist has obtained this information, the client is brought to a spiritual standpoint from which to start gaining enlightenment. The client is advised to look for his or her guardian angels, spiritual guides, the masters, the light, or their higher selves to help answer additional and equally important questions.

The first of these questions the therapist counsels the client to ask their spiritual guide is: *What was your lesson in that life?*

The next question is: *What is your lesson in your present life?* Knowing *this* life's lesson allows the client the opportunity to address the issue and complete the lesson so they do not have to continue learning the lesson germane to that particular issue.

Connecting Past to Present

Through this specific, gentle, and profound process, the reader will be able to follow the client reaching a state of awareness or connection between their past and present lives. In this awareness or connection, the client finds the answer to their intention within their story and comes to understand how that story plays a role in their story of this present life.

At that point, the client and the therapist discuss the insights and develop methods to resolve the triggering issue and integrate whatever is necessary into his or her life.

Recognizing Our Soul Group

As part of this revelatory process, a client is also able to tell who the people are from their past life in *this* life. Identifying people in this way is called recognizing our soul circles or soul group. For example, our mother in a past life could be our daughter in this life. We may be a father to another soul in our soul group in one life and a brother in a different life. A child of an individual in one life may be a parent or a grandparent to that person in another. We identify these people by their energy rather than by their exact physical attributes. They may *feel* like our daughter here, have the same smile, or have that special twinkle in the eye. We later make the connection of who is whom, which adds understanding about our relationships with them in this life.

There are also times we may remember cellularly the life drama of one from our soul group and channel an archetypal energy to learn what we are supposed to learn from them. The change or healing is just as effective.

We, too, may manifest differently from past lives to our present life and even have different roles and genders. Perhaps we have children in one life but not in another. Male and female bodies may switch around.

Releasing Negative Energetic Blockages

All throughout the regression, the therapist helps the client release any negative emotions from the past life that could have developed into energetic, emotional blocks in this life. This clearing is done with breath work and visualization. Releasing this energy is what helps transform an issue or illness into clarity and wellness.

After working with so many clients, the author is always amazed—but never surprised—at the profound healing that occurs on so many levels as the emotions are released and connections to the present life are made. Other regressionists report the same experience, concurring that once the client understands what he or she needs to do to clear their Karma and fulfill their life lesson(s), the client's sense of purpose is renewed.

As the old *Karma* is cleared, new *Karma* is created. Since we build new Karma with our thoughts, words, and actions, we must be careful about what we want — or do not want — to create once we start moving into our future.

My Journey into Past-Life Work

Strangely, I was not gasping for air. My lungs were not filling, and my arms were not flailing. Instead, I stood peacefully on the bottom of the pool. As if with an invisible hand, the water had pulled me down, submerged me, and covered me.

What was happening? Why could I not float and swim like the other eight-year-olds at the camp? They had made it look so easy, the way they jumped off the diving board at the deep end, executing the swan jumps and flips and the oh-so-funny belly flops.

But when I jumped in, I splashed and then went down.

As I stood on the concrete bottom, I saw a cloud overhead and a woman reaching down to me. In my calm, I tried to understand who she was. It seemed like I was pondering this question for hours, but it had to be only seconds. I heard angelic, soft music, and I thought: *I'm not going with her; my mother always taught me not to go with strangers.*

Still standing on the bottom of the pool, I glanced over to the ladder. Through the water, I saw feet kicking above and from behind. I felt the strong arms of a lifeguard scoop me up and carry me to the surface. I looked behind me for the woman, but she was gone. I kept scanning the surface of the water for the woman, but I never saw her face again.

I did not need resuscitation. I simply walked away. Some of my friends thought I had been teasing.

Upon returning home, I shared this experience with my mother. She admonished me for going into the deep end of the pool not knowing how to swim and accused the camp of being dangerously irresponsible. She accused me of watching too much television. She told me to forget the woman in the clouds and the angelic music.

Then she whispered, "Don't tell anyone else, Cindy, or they'll think you're crazy." It was 1959, and this sort of thing was not deemed normal and, therefore, was not acceptable. I did not mention it to my mother again—or to anyone else, for that matter.

Ten years later, in college, I was drawn to a book called *Life After Life*. The author's name, Raymond Moody, meant nothing to me, but the title and the subject drew me in immediately.

Life after life. Raymond Moody had interviewed those who had had near-death experiences, and many of the interviewees described loved ones or angels like mine reaching down to people in times of great need or emotional stress. He offered many examples of similar experiences, all of which taught there was no real finality, only new beginnings. After reading this book, I was able to define my episode as a near-death experience.

Since that day at the pool, I had always felt very close to and compatible with nature. I had an easy rapport with people; they turned to me for guidance, and I felt acutely, intuitively sensitive to their needs. I went through college and graduate school with a strong desire to help and heal people and was fascinated with human nature and psychology. I choose the path of special education and received a master's degree in that field.

It was the late 1960s and early '70s, a time when the established order and rules of parents and the older generation in general were slowly giving way. Minds were altering, both from chemical input and from influences from the East. The Beatles were introducing Maharishi Mahesh Yogi, and Cat Stevens was becoming a Sufi. R.D. Laing was presenting a new kind of psychology, and the primal scream was "in." Carlos Castaneda was required reading, and writers like Edgar Cayce and Rudolph Steiner were acquiring a newfound respectability.

I was magnetically drawn to paranormal psychology, talking to psychics, participating in workshops, conferences, seeking out my rabbi and other religious leaders. My experience as an eight-year-old had stayed with me. I continued to read every book I could find on the subject of death and dying (or not dying). I read "paranormal" psychology books, volumes on channeling, psychic phenomenon, experiments in Russia, religion, reincarnation, and, finally, Past Life Regression therapy.

It was a relatively new discipline but one that connected my heart to my gut. The only way I could begin my studies was to practice regressions with a tape recorder on myself, family, and friends who would allow me.

I was turning what might have started as a curiosity into something meaningful and powerful, uncovering astonishing information and concluding with deep, healing results.

The picture became clearer, threads emerged; connections from past lifetimes, important pieces, as of a puzzle, helped me understand the present lifetime.

Everything I learned came naturally and felt right. The spiritual knowledge was enlightening and validating, providing a sense of fulfillment that I had not felt in my more traditional education. Lingering questions were slowly, but certainly, being answered.

Eventually, I felt the responsibility to formalize my training and obtain certification. I went back to school, became a certified Ericksonian hypnotherapist, and entered another master's program for social work counseling. I never finished this master's program as it was too similar to my first master's degree. Besides, it had no relevance to Past Life Regressions.

All these efforts were important steps for me, but something was still missing. I knew deep within my core that I was not paying proper attention to the discoveries and intuitive skills that were emerging from my informal work with Past Life Regression. I was aware of a deeper consciousness, other lives, and other realms. A desire was wakening to devote myself to these other lives, to those other realms that were speaking to me with such vigor and coherence.

It's either meant to be or it's not, I thought, listening to the synchronicities (or, as I call them, "non-coincidences"). These synchronicities seemed to be guiding me like an invisible hand, a hand very similar to the one that led me to safety in the pool that day years before.

"Go with your gut or knowingness," was the message of the day, and it was not lost on me. I pursued the path, gaining greater confidence with each step forward. I joined a professional organization, The Association for Past Life Research and Therapy, leading and participating in workshops given by leading regression therapists, sharing experiences and techniques. I was astounded to see results that validated for me everything on this path. I got to share the experiences of others and to test my own.

I was fascinated to see that, far from being a new, innovative science, Past Life Regression had a long and noble history, as deep and rich as our dream life and as memorable as the archetypes of our existence. The multitude of psychiatrists, psychologists, social workers, healers of all kinds, and spiritual leaders using this therapy in their practices surprised me.

However, it was still a closet science, and we all felt a sense of vulnerability. How could we be sure? How could we define our methodology and at the same time establish our credibility in a world of the material, the scientific, the ultra-rational, and ultimately non-experiential? Many were keeping it quiet, fearful of risking reputations that had taken so long to establish.

Yet the iceberg was moving. A tremendous shift was underway in ourselves (this was the age of a new millennium, after all) and in the psyche of our very planet. We all started finding many, many more people open to such findings, and many clinicians were experiencing, chronicling, and validating the same phenomena.

The most important element in all this was the increased speed in healing the client. What could have taken years of traditional psychotherapy was being accomplished sometimes within weeks! We were not abandoning old systems; rather, we were absorbing the new, and the results were spectacular. We saw amazing healings on many levels—including physical ones—as emotions were released and connections made from the past to the present life.

The discipline known as Past Life Regression therapy grew from a tiny group of practitioners to a well-respected and fast-growing field worldwide. People seeking connections, healings, and to repair psychic wounds—or wounds to the psyche—found help with Past Life Regression therapy. This therapy has been found helpful for almost everything, whether mental, spiritual, physical, emotional, or energetic in nature. Now, there are therapists practicing all over the world just in the professional association alone.

As I continued my work, many themes, lessons, and theologies blossomed. Important information emerged that mankind needs to know. This book represents what a sacred tool this work is to my clients and which was such an important step in my own spiritual growth.

I now seek not only to share this illumination, the timely stories, and spiritual knowledge, but to help pull together what it is we all need to learn from this information. For me, life is unfolding as a script that we put together before entering our physical body, one that will help us understand what we need to learn, with whom we need to learn it, and the choices that can always change our past, present, and future Karma.

We need to know who we were in order to better understand who we are. In this constant process of remembering our pasts, there comes a shedding of our bodies, a cycle of incarnation into other lives and bodies all drawn together by a miraculous spiritual flow. Science is only beginning to define and quantify that spiritual flow that the spirit has known all along. We have the tools within us to know this spiritual flow: prayer, the unconscious, an open heart and mind, a power, and wonder that can cross lifetimes and dimensions.

We are all the same people, each sharing the same breath from the Supreme Being that has given us life. We have all been the victim and the abuser. We have all been Chinese, African, Jewish, Catholic, handicapped, or kingly. Therefore, we need not judge others since we have been where they are now or will be.

We have forgotten how to live our basic truths of how to love, be at peace, and live in harmony with humans, animals, and the environment that nourishes and shelters us. Our greatest obstacle is how to get there. Our greatest barrier is intolerance—both of others and of the beauty within ourselves.

Near-death experiences reported around the world indicate that when we leave this world, we are our own judges. We witness a life review and know where we have failed to learn, where we have created good, and what we must do to compensate for our missteps. We know that we will walk into the next life better prepared, with greater wisdom, and with greater experience, but we must remember why we have come and what we must do to achieve our lesson.

It is up to us to accept without judgment the lives we have led, trusting that we chose this life in order to learn and thereby to bring ourselves closer to the Oneness that we know as God.

I share my stories hoping that something in them may touch what *you* need to learn while on your spiritual journey.

You are reading this book because you already know all of this. Now is the time to act on it.

~ Saundra C. Blum
Katonah, New York

CHAPTER ONE

Relationships and Soul Mates

Instantly, we arrive into this life with our connections to mother, father, and God. Later in life, we move toward other intimate relationships, marriage, children, and grandchildren. During our life, we meet people with whom we feel an instant closeness or instant connection or bond because, most likely, we have known them from another life.

What we are experiencing are cellular memories from those lifetimes. Chapter One contains eight lifetimes with the type of relationships that we have all experienced. Some of these relationships are warm and loving, and some are abusive.

Through the memories of my clients' lives, the reader is able to understand that the reasons we have to experience both the good and what we consider "bad" relationships is either to teach or learn from them—or both and to clear karma. The reader will also learn the meaning of the term "soul mate."

Relationships

A Broken Heart

Linda came to my office to see me after she found out her husband had been cheating on her for most of their marriage.

"I just can't trust my husband!"

Intention:

Let's go back to a lifetime that is at the core of your trust issues with your husband.

Linda regressed back to a lifetime in France in the late 1600s, seeing herself as a lovely, young French girl in ornate clothing and surroundings. As an only child in that lifetime, she was bored and spoiled. She lived in a palatial home with cold, self-centered parents. Her parents kept up with their social circle by giving parties during which they would barely interact with their daughter. She had everything one could want—except love. Linda's only companion and love in her life was her horse, with which she spent many hours.

As Linda reported on her relationship with her parents, her speech slowed, and her look became sullen.

We released that sadness and the feelings of isolation and abandonment she was feeling at that moment. I used a visualization process and breath work to remove energetically the negative emotions causing the blockage.

I could see a lightness come over her. Her coloring changed. Her muscle tension dissipated, and I felt light fill the space around her. We continued.

As I progressed Linda, I could see the loneliness form in her facial muscles. She folded her arms around herself in a loving manner, giving herself something that she had not gotten from anyone in that life.

I progressed her in five-year intervals, and she was either alone or with her horse. She detached from her pain by creating fantasies of romance, love, and travel.

When Linda was eighteen, her parents threw a ball so that she could meet her future husband. He was a society man who was cruel and non-caring. He was not the gallant knight of her fantasies, and she felt sad and powerless. She could not love this man, making the engagement silly in her eyes. But she had to honor the formalities of the time and marry the suitor her parents chose.

Sitting in the hypnosis chair, her eyebrows lowered; her voice became louder and stronger. Her anger grew at the thought of marrying someone she disliked so intensely. As a therapist and empath, I also felt this anger; my client's freedom of choice had not been honored. I helped her release more anger, sadness, and helplessness.

As her father ordered, Linda married this cruel man. Whenever she could, she would sneak off to the stables to be with her horse.

Over time, she developed a friendship with the stable boy, Jonathan. He was sympathetic and reassuring, and, against all the conventions of the time, she fell in love with the empathetic stable boy. She did not, however, have the courage to run off with her lover.

They continued to meet over the next five years before Jonathan realized that Linda could never be his. He told her that continuing this relationship had become too torturous, and so he left. Eventually, Jonathan found a woman with whom he fell in love and married. When he moved away, Linda's heart broke.

I watched and listened to Linda sobbing in the hypnosis chair. I helped her release her sadness through breath work.

As time went on, Linda grew even more distant from her husband, who never knew about her affair. And since there were many ladies of the court willing to be of service to him, he did not mind Linda's lack of affection.

The years wore on, and Linda often thought of her stable boy and the love they had shared. She grew depressed and very alone, isolating herself from everyone and everything.

As Linda explained how her continual thoughts of the love she had shared with the stable boy brought her into depression and isolation, she began shrinking in the chair. She held herself, seeking to comfort the despair while explaining how she wished to achieve peace. "Please let me die," she sobbed.

Her feelings were so intense, I had to use visualization to help her release these emotions. The Linda of the 1600s died at age fifty of a broken heart.

Last Thoughts:

I miss the stable boy. I am so alone and just want to die.

Lesson:

Love and strength

Awareness and Connection:

In that past life, Linda and her husband had cheated on each other. Due to infidelity by both parties, they needed to work out that Karma now. Her husband in her current life had been her husband in that lifetime, too. The intensity of their Karma in this lifetime was deepened by a loveless marriage in which both parties were unfaithful. In order to clear this Karma, they needed to either stay faithful or walk away by divorcing.

Because Linda had not married out of love in this lifetime either, she had to learn the same lesson she had learned in the other life: namely, how to love her husband or find and keep real love with someone else.

Linda's guides advised us that there were seven past lives to investigate in order to clear her Karma concerning the issue of infidelity. We set up several appointments so we could regress back to those seven lifetimes and release them.

Relationships

<u>Forever Cursed</u>

Edward came to see me to understand why he had come into this life with his abusive mother. She was angry with him since he could remember, even when he was a little boy. She made him feel whatever he did was not good enough and oddly enough that he never spent enough time at home with her. He felt he was always home with her until he went away to college.

"My mother has been abusive and mean-spirited to me ever since I can remember."

Intention:

Let us go back to the life that will help you understand why your mother has been mean-spirited to you in this life.

Edward returned to a lifetime as a young boy of twelve in England in the early 1700s. He found himself standing on a dock "where tall ships were anchored," describing their splendor, imagining their great adventures, imaging that one day he would be part of those great adventures.

Progressed to twenty years of age, Edward married Mary, a beautiful but prim and proper Englishwoman who demanded more of his time than he was willing to give. When Mary complained, "You are never home with your family," or "You never help around the house," Edward's response to her whining was to hit her.

Becoming a sailor not only fulfilled Edward's dream, but he was also able to get away from Mary. He left to go off adventuring to different, far-away countries for extended periods of time. He hated returning home, and Mary was glad when he left.

On one of his visits home, Mary became pregnant. By age thirty, they had two children, and the only emotions between him and Mary were anger, hate, and resentment. Finally, Edward sailed off on a voyage, never to return to Mary and their children.

At forty years of age, Edward developed an illness from his travels to exotic lands. After suffering with a high fever, he died alone.

Later, when he went to the spirit side, Edward learned that Mary had cursed him daily because of his lack of love, abuse, and abandonment of her.

Last Thoughts:

Sorry he married so early before traveling to the lands about which he had dreamed.

Lesson:

Responsibility

Awareness and Connection:

Edward's mother in this life had been his wife, Mary, in that past life. His children in that life are also his children in this life. Describing his mother, he stated, "She is still alive and still angry." Now understanding the cause of his mother's anger, he was able to forgive her.

I suggested that he share this story with his mother as a possible healing tool for her. Months later, he reported that he did, but "she said she didn't believe in past lives." However, after he told her about their prior life, she has been considerably nicer to him.

Relationships

<u>Bitterly Alone</u>

Cynthia came to see me due to her depression and loneliness. When I was getting her history, she explained that her father left when she was a small child and that she felt it was her fault. She explained that he probably didn't want children, and with her being born it broke the marriage. She said she wished she were never born.

"I always wondered if my dad leaving us when I was a child was my fault."

Intention:

Let's go back to the lifetime that brought you into this life to experience your father leaving you as a small child.

Cynthia regressed back to New Hampshire in the year 1890. In that lifetime, Cynthia was a male named Michael. She seemed surprised as she described herself wearing big, black shoes, black trousers, and a loose-fitting white shirt with hair down to her shoulders.

She was eighteen when she first saw herself in the library of her home, a room that included a fireplace. She said, "I feel happy in that room yet feel a deep sadness inside."

I asked Michael to find his mother. He replied that she had died at childbirth. He showed little emotion as he related his childhood, including his being raised by his father as an only child. Michael blamed his father's cold and distant attitude on his mother's death.

As I progressed Michael forward to twenty-five years of age, he reported that he had married and had a child. His wife was beautiful but also emotionally distant. He tried to get close to her, but she, too, had had an emotionally deprived childhood. This made Michael angry.

Cynthia's facial expression changed into an angry smirk. She kept shifting her body in the chair.

Jealous of the relationship Michael's wife had with their child, he hid his resentment in his work as a farmer.

I progressed Michael to thirty. Not much had changed. He felt isolated from his family and continued to throw himself into his work. Progressed to forty, Cynthia started to cry. When I asked why, she responded as Michael, "My child died from influenza."

Instead of that bringing his wife closer to him, she became more withdrawn, insolating herself from Michael even more.

Progressing ahead to forty-five years of age, Michael reported his wife died from a broken heart. He said she refused to eat, talk, or sleep. "She finally got what she really wanted—to be with our daughter."

As I progressed Michael to fifty, he described himself as "bitterly alone." Feeling that life was just too hard, he hung himself.

Last Thoughts:

Life is just too sad and lonely. What's the point?

Lesson:

Strength

Awareness and Connection:

I explained to Cynthia that life as Michael was constantly testing him to learn that life lesson—strength. Michael's test was one of abandonment, which began with losing his mother during childbirth, having his father withdraw, choosing an emotionally vacant wife, and then finally losing his child.

Instead of dealing with his emotions and desires, Michael threw himself into his work. He finally took his life as he could no longer continue to suffer the pain and loneliness and no longer felt he had a reason to live.

Whenever we take our life or just give up, we almost always come into this life feeling the same suicidal tendencies. Cynthia confirmed her own suicidal feelings and was grateful that she finally understood from where they came.

Michael's lack of strength in that life led to his inability to face his feelings and work things out. Cynthia's lesson in this life is also strength. She scripted her life so that her father would leave (instead of her mother in the past life) so that she could learn the same lesson of strength around the issue of abandonment.

She no longer blames herself for being so bad that she did not deserve love. Understanding the bigger picture enables her to love her father and herself. And she vows to learn her lesson of strength in this lifetime so that she will not have to repeat it.

Relationships

No Time Alone

Fran came to see me after she adopted a Chinese baby. She felt very connected to her baby as soon as she met her.

It made her wonder if they may have known each other from another life. She asked if I felt she could have been a biological mother to her before this life.

"Could my adopted Chinese daughter have been a biological child in my past life?"

Intention:

Let us go back to the life you shared with Karen when you were her biological mother. Or if you were not her mother, then let us go to the life that brought you and Karen together in this one.

Fran was excited as she sat in the hypnosis chair. She regressed into a life in the mid-1800s in Georgia (USA), where she saw herself as Becky holding Karen shortly after she had given birth to her. Fran sat in the hypnosis chair crying, both as Becky crying in joy over the birth of her new baby but also as Fran crying tears of soul recognition that she and Karen had been biologically joined in that previous lifetime.

Fran explained that Becky and her husband had tried repeatedly to have this little girl and that "nothing" would ever come between them. Becky had married George (also Fran's husband in this lifetime) at age sixteen, and they had wanted to have children immediately. However, George had had a problem that had caused scar tissue to form in his penis, resulting in difficulty in producing hardy sperm. Finally after much praying and trying, Becky became pregnant and was eighteen when she gave birth to Karen.

Progressed to age twenty-five, Becky continued to dote on Karen. She loved combing Karen's long, beautiful, blond hair and tying it up with bows. She baked cookies with Karen, played with her, took long walks with her, and taught her how to read and pray—since it was prayer that had brought Karen to her.

Fran smiled continuously as she gave her account of that time. And I realized I was smiling with her. Becky reported that during that period, "We are so happy and busy with Karen, we hardly have time alone anymore."

I progressed Becky to age thirty. Karen was now twelve and moody. Fran told me that Karen did not like her mother doting on her so much and that she needed "her own time" to be alone and plan what she wanted to do. However, Becky started having separation anxiety. She would only allow Karen ten minutes of alone time every three hours. Karen started to resent both her mother and her father for "trying to control her life."

At thirteen, Karen ran away from home to both get away from her parents and to see the world. Becky and George were devastated and blamed each other for her disappearance.

After a torturous six months of hoping and waiting, Becky and George set out to find their daughter. They made their journey in a horse and wagon. On the third day of their journey, the horse stumbled as it was trotting. The wagon tipped over, crushing Becky and George to death.

Fran has complained of arthritis in her back and knees in this life. I used visualization to pull out the energy of the trauma of that accident and the sadness from the loss of her daughter.

Last Thoughts:

Since her death was quick, she had had no time for last thoughts.

Lesson:

Independence

Awareness and Connection:

Fran was correct in thinking that her adopted daughter in this life had been her biological daughter in another lifetime. As she came out of her trance, crying, her first words were, "I guess I will have to let go and give her space to grow in this life."

Since being an adoptive child is also a choice that souls make, Karen may have chosen to return as an adopted child due to her parents' over-possessiveness in their past life.

Another issue that was resolved for Fran was fear about sexual intercourse. The stress of physiological interference from their past life and then letting go of something special made out of love resulted in not being able to conceive in this life. She remembered her husband had held a lot of guilt about both his own sexual dysfunction and Karen's leaving. This time, it was Fran who was sexually dysfunctional, helping her to learn more compassion for George for his dysfunction in their past life. This is a good example of karmic balance.

Since our soul group travels together, even adopted children are not coincidental and may have been part of our biological family in the past.

Relationships

Together Again

On a cold winter day, a week after an evening workshop, Samantha came to my office with the question she had asked at our prior meeting: "Do you think I could be my Aunt Rose?" She explained her aunt had died before Samantha was born, and although the family rarely spoke about Aunt Rose, her aunts frequently commented how much Samantha reminded them of Rose in looks and manner. Samantha brought a picture of Aunt Rose, which showed a remarkable resemblance between the two. Further, from the time Samantha was a child, she liked taking afternoon tea with her aunts—much as Rose had also enjoyed the same. We were both excited about the possibility that Samantha had been Aunt Rose in a prior life.

Samantha apologized for not knowing much about her aunt, explaining that the family, particularly Samantha's father, felt uncomfortable talking about Aunt Rose. All Samantha knew about Rose was that they looked alike and had the same mannerisms. Rose had died young, but the family never talked about the details.

While listening to Samantha, I wondered what her father would think if he found out that his deceased sister was now his daughter? I also wondered why Samantha chose him as a parent rather than choosing one of her other aunts. What was the Karma they had to work through that brought them into this parent-child relationship?

"Do you think I could be my deceased aunt?"

Intention:

Let us go back to the past to see if you were your father's sister, Aunt Rose, who died before you were born.

Samantha regressed to 1950, the year in which Aunt Rose was born. In this life, Samantha was born in 1975.

When Rose was born, Samantha reported seeing her other aunts, Rose's sisters, gathered around the cradle staring at the newborn. Samantha saw that her father, Rose's brother, did not join his sisters around the cradle but instead was sitting alone in a corner.

I progressed Samantha to the age of five, when Aunt Rose's sisters surrounded her in a summerhouse. In a child's voice, she described the fun she had swimming in the lake, attending family picnics, and playing games. When the summer ended, she did not want to leave.

I asked Samantha what her name was in that life. She said "Rose." She continued telling me of a small pond in which she and her brother would catch frogs and race them.

I progressed her to the age of ten, but, instead, Samantha went to the age of twelve. She grabbed her stomach, wincing in pain and crying for help as she sat in my hypnosis chair.

Samantha saw herself as Rose rushed from her summer home to the local hospital. There, the doctors performed an emergency appendectomy just in time, preventing its rupturing and her possible death. The recuperation period took two weeks.

At fifteen years old, Samantha fell in love with Rick, the most wonderful boy she had ever met. He was kind and gentle yet strong and handsome. Likewise, Rick thought Samantha was the most wonderful girl he had ever met. Both hoped their summer would never end. After the summer finally did come to a close, they wrote back and forth, pledging their love and their future together forever.

Progressed to her sixteenth birthday, Samantha sat in the hypnosis chair stiff and barely able to move. She explained that Rose was now stricken with polio and paralyzed from the waist down. But her condition did not prevent Rick from continuing to pledge his undying love.

Samantha felt guilty, however, about tying Rick down with a cripple. But Rick's loyalty and love did not waver, and he remained constant.

Samantha cringed in the chair, recalling the horrific pain and muscle cramps. As Aunt Rose, Samantha tried to be what she considered to be a trooper to hide her pain from Rick, but he could see through her façade.

That year, Rose died from polio.

Last Thoughts:

Holding Rick's hand, Rose told him, "Don't worry; we will be together again someday." In turn, Rick pledged faithfulness and love.

Lesson:

Self-love

Awareness and Connection:

Believing that her crippled legs in that lifetime made her ugly, Samantha carried self-esteem issues into the present life, thinking that people in this life also believe she is ugly. Instantly, Samantha understood why she always felt that way in this life. We were both hopeful that this would help her to understand her feelings and to let go of the energy around it. With time, Samantha did learn to love herself and did start to feel more confident.

After the first session, Samantha went home and asked her father whether Aunt Rose had had an appendectomy and whether she had had excruciating leg pain due to polio. She was also curious about what had happened to Rick in that life. Was he still alive? And had he remained true to his pledge to love her forever?

Samantha's father confirmed what she had learned in her regression. Aunt Rose had had an appendicitis, and she was crippled and in pain from the polio that later caused her death. He was surprised that Samantha knew about the appendicitis, something he had forgotten until reminded.

Her father expressed his remorse about not spending much time with Rose. She had spent most of her time with his sisters. Samantha, as Rose, also regretted not spending enough time with her brother. But now as father and daughter, they could finally have that time together, thus fulfilling their Karma.

Samantha found out that Rick had never married, and she wondered if he was waiting to see her again in their next life. She thought about visiting him to see if he would recognize her. She also wanted to see if love traveled over space and time. What was the effect of the mutual pledge between Rose and Rick to love each other and be together forever?

Upon further contemplation, Samantha decided not to look for Rick, Rose's lost love, who was now her father's age. She reasoned that meeting her might upset him.

Relationships

Such a Talented Wife

Deborah sat with me and discussed her anger toward her husband, Jake. Her face was rigid and drawn. Deborah's husband was a well-known music artist who was highly respected in the music field.

Deborah knew this when she married him. However, she felt he would help her rise in her own musical career. While Deborah's work did keep getting better, it was not due to any help from her husband.

When they were with prominent music people or even just friends, everyone continued to make a big deal out of Jake and his music. Deborah always remained in the shadows. Her self-esteem was low, and her anger and resentment kept building.

"I feel like I am a shadow of my husband; no one notices my music."

Intention:

Let us go back to the life that brought you into this life feeling like you are only a shadow of your husband, especially in your music.

I regressed Deborah back to a lifetime in ancient Persia. She was one of many wives in a harem. She said she was the favorite of her master, for she was the most beautiful and most talented. Even back then, Deborah had a wonderful voice. She often would sing for her master and his company. The other wives were very jealous due to her popularity. Deborah looked very sad.

When I regressed Deborah back to her youth in that lifetime to see how her life manifested, she saw herself at ten years old being auctioned for sale in the slave market. Her family needed the money, so they sold their daughter to this man who could provide a "better" life for her.

As we progressed to age fifteen, we saw Deborah in a struggle with this man, for he would be rough with her in bed and out. Deborah started screaming, "Leave me alone! Don't hurt me!" If Deborah dared to speak out in self-defense, she would be whipped. She hated this master, whom she identified as her husband in this life. Deborah started crying in my chair at the hopelessness she felt. I jumped at the chance to help her release these feelings.

In the Persian past life, I regressed Deborah to age twenty, when she continued to perform. She left her body often in that period in order to deal with the traumas she had to endure from her husband. Even when she performed, her master was given the credit for owning such a talented wife. Finally, Deborah could take it no longer and hung herself in the palace.

Lesson:

To use her voice

Last Thoughts:

Deborah's last thoughts were of only wanting to leave that life, hoping the next would be better.

Awareness and Connection:

Deborah picked up a lot of connections. In this life, due to the music bond and hope that her husband would help her career, Deborah always felt owned or in debt to her husband. Likewise, in her past life, Deborah also felt owned or in debt to her husband. Similarly, Deborah's talents were not acknowledged as hers but as the wisdom of her master for owning such a wife. Again, she felt like a shadow to her master with her musical gift.

Deborah was also able to make a new connection. In this life, she had always been fearful of her husband in bed. Yet in this life, he was always very gentle. Deborah realized she carried that fear from the previous lifetime, and we were able to release it.

One last and very important piece of information given to us from Deborah's guide was that *Deborah's husband was her split soul*. They were here to mirror each other. She asked her guide if she should leave Jake, and the guide replied, "No, you are here to support each other in your respective work."

Since Deborah's lesson was to "speak her voice," she knew that to survive and end her repeated abusive Karma, she needed to "speak her voice" to Jake — to speak up for herself, promote herself, and to respect and love herself.

Deborah thanked me for helping her gain her power back, to understand who she really is, and why she always felt this shadow persona. The irony is that Deborah has such a beautiful voice, and yet her lesson was about using it for self-protection and empowerment.

When, for protection, we leave our bodies as Deborah had as the suffering wife with her master, occasionally our soul may split and leave. I had asked Deborah if this had happened, and she said it had. I helped Deborah call back her split soul to join the rest of her soul to become whole once again.

Relationships

We Are All One

Wendy came to my office laughing at her problem. "I feel so silly coming here for this, but I like Paul, and he has been a great resource and mentor for me. I just get a deep pit in my stomach and anger every time we get up in front of our group and Paul begins to speak. He is a PhD and seems to identify his self-worth with his education, which sometimes makes others in our group feel less worthy.

It could just be my own perception, but I get furious by the end of the evening. Usually, I would just slough it off as his own need to feel worthy, but I can't. I must see where this is coming from."

I asked Wendy, "How did you feel when you first met him?" She responded that she felt she could depend on him and that she has enjoyed his friendship and their mutual respect.

"Why do I feel so angry with this colleague whenever we speak in front of a group we facilitate?"

Intention:

Let us go back to the life that brought you into this life feeling so angry every time you speak in front of a group that you facilitate with your colleague Paul.

I regressed Wendy back to a very special lifetime for her. She went back to ancient Essenes. She came up as a young boy crouching in the sand and drawing a letter or character over and over. She thought her name was Aaron or something close to it.

Aaron loved drawing letters, approaching it almost as an art. He also started to draw fish. When I asked why fish, he responded, "The fish represents that to which we are all trying to evolve. It has come here in unconditional love and sacrifice. We revere fish since fish came here to nourish us so that we may eat it and grow as a community. Likewise, we need to become as evolved, to learn unconditional love and sacrifice for each other, for that is what is good for the whole. There is no 'I,' for we are all one."

I thought, *Wow*! How exciting to hear the true meaning of what later was to become a symbol for Christ.

I asked Aaron about his family. He had a father whom he loved and respected deeply. His trade was that of a pottery craftsman. Wendy thought he was her husband, Bob, in this life. Bob loves to make pottery here in this life as well.

I progressed her to fifteen years old, where she saw herself as a donkey-packer. She would pack people's donkeys with things they needed to bring for travel to other cities. I asked why that job, and she responded, "We are given or choose jobs that we can do well. I can pack donkeys well. No one here is any better or worse than the other, for we are all God's children. If we need to be something, we can. If we are good at something, we can do that. We have no 'ego' we call 'self' here, for that is a sin. Remember there is no 'I'; it is always what is good for us."

I progressed Wendy to age twenty, where she was arguing with her parents about a beautiful woman Aaron wanted to take as his bride.

"What seems to be the problem with taking this woman as your bride?" I asked.

Wendy stated, "My parents were warning me about her beauty, since she could get into 'self.'" Despite his parents' warning, Aaron married this woman.

When I regressed him to age twenty-five, they had two children. Aaron seemed to be quite agitated, for he saw his parents' prophecies coming true. His wife spent many hours each day looking into her mirror, painting her face, and fixing her hair. Aaron realized his wife had sinned, and he had to share this with the elders for the protection of their community.

The elders agreed that this might "taint" the community. So it was Aaron's responsibility to God and his community to donkey-pack her out of town. Aaron was surprised at the lack of emotion he felt sending his wife off to other lands. Aaron loved her, but his first responsibility to the group or community was to protect "the laws of God," which were greater than one single love in a family.

Again, I marveled at the richness of this information. The wife was Paul, Wendy's colleague. Wendy had many more significant revelations during this regression, too many to describe here.

Lesson:

Truth

Awareness and Connection:

Wendy now understands from where her anger came. The attitude Paul expresses in front of the group brings up the cellular memory of what a sin it was to be in "self" or ego, that we are all the same regardless of whether we are donkey-packers or PhDs. We are all God's children.

We do what we need to do here in order to learn our lessons. Wendy now understands the need to stand in her "truth" of who and what she is. She also now understands why her spiritual quest and work are so important to her. She stands in the truth that no one is any better than the next person, that we are all one.

She has forgiven Paul for holding on to remnants of that ego as Wendy's wife in the previous life. She no longer has that anger when they come in front of the group. She and others are teaching Paul to be more humble. He has also been teaching Wendy and others his knowledge from the past and the present.

Relationships

<u>She Needs to Help People</u>

As a teenager, my son, Jordan, always hated my past-life regression therapy healing practice, saying it was like voodoo and asking,

Why can't you be like all the other mothers?

Intention:

This regression came about spontaneously.

I was having a massage and listening to Native American music, particularly enjoying the drums and flutes. All of a sudden, I had an image of a Native American Indian who was wearing a fur jacket with a fur hood standing beside a woman in the same type of clothing, whom I assumed to be his wife. In that instant, I knew that these two people were my parents in that life. Further, I realized that the man (my father in that life) was my son in this one and that the woman beside him (my mother in that life) was now my daughter, Briana.

In the next image, I saw myself, a young, bare-chested, strong, handsome brave. I had a knowing that we were a bear-hunting tribe, which meant my responsibility was to hunt bears.

However, loving the woods and animals, I was strongly opposed to hunting. Instead, I wanted to go into the woods to collect flowers and leaves and turn them into medicine. This desire outraged and shamed my parents, who wanted their son to be a great bear hunter in the tradition of the tribe. I heard my father in that life lament, "Why can't you be like all the other braves?" This echoed the feelings of my son in this life, who wanted me to fit into the norm.

Even though I eventually became a great medicine man, I was a joke to my father. When my father was on his death bed, I tried to heal him, still hoping to save his life and win his approval. I worked on him for days, but, by then, the illness was too far progressed, and he died despite my efforts.

Last Thoughts:

My father's last words were, "You think you're such a healer, but your medicine can't save me." He left in anger and shame.

Lesson:

My father's lesson was about tolerance. Mine was standing in my truth.

Awareness and Connection:

I finally understood why my son was extremely angry about my work and why my not being "like all the other mothers" was so important.

I shared this story with my son, thinking it would help him understand his feelings. He listened with resistance.

Two weeks later, I was driving with my son and daughter. My daughter, who is both spiritual and tolerant, seemed to be experiencing separation anxiety and was upset about my attending a workshop that evening. Much to my surprise, my son told his sister with great sincerity that I had to go to the workshop because I needed to help people.

I was astounded at this change of attitude. Although my son has never been comfortable with my work in Past Life Regression, he has become tolerant. In telling him the story of this past life in which he had a similar attitude, I had planted the seeds of understanding, which led to acceptance, thereby removing his anger and shame.

Further, the memory of that lifetime removed my own guilt about my work and allowed me to step into my full power as a healer without fear of losing my family. Sometimes, just sharing your regression with the person in it can help that person to understand and release negative emotions without going through the past life under hypnosis.

Relationships

Gratitude

Barbara arrived at my office excited because of a new doctor she had just met. In private sessions, they acknowledged the feelings between them as soul love. The love they both felt for their spouses, however, did not prevent them from feeling intense attraction to one another.

"How can I love my husband and still feel attracted to the new doctor who is treating my family?"

Intention:

Let us go back to the lifetime that brought you and this doctor into this life together to understand your Karma.

I regressed Barbara to a life in a small town in Mongolia, where she and her husband lived. Both of them had an uneventful childhood. Barbara, Rae in that life, had a sense of constant fear of neighboring terrorists. As she was speaking with me, she was hiding under the blanket, shaking as she spoke.

I progressed Barbara to the age of twenty, where she saw herself terrified by hordes of terrorists on horseback surrounding her home. Rae and her husband were tied at the wrists and ankles and hung upside down and transported on a long stick. Holding her hands as if they were bound, Barbara winced in pain. The worst part of the experience was that she and her husband witnessed the killing of their young daughter.

At this time, we worked on Barbara, releasing the fear and sadness from watching her daughter's murder.

Rae and her husband's lives were spared. Because of Rae's beauty, the terrorist leader took her away from her husband,

and her husband was put to work as a slave in the mines. Occasionally, Rae would see him.

The terrorist leader dressed her in the finest material, gave her beautiful jewels, and fed her the finest food. Instead of hating him for what he did to her child and husband, she grew to return his love.

This made her husband angry that his wife, lavished with gifts, seemed to forsake their daughter. Rae became pregnant with the child of her new husband, the soul of her murdered child reincarnated as her second child, who came back to be reunited with her mother in her mother's new and better life.

Although Rae's life was happy, upon her death, she carried feelings of guilt and sadness around the death of her first child and treatment of her first husband.

Rae's first husband in that life remained angry with her because she was happy with her second husband and new daughter. In this life, when Barbara's husband met the new doctor, Barbara's husband was confused with what he thought were unjustified feelings of jealousy and anger that surfaced.

Last Thoughts:

I am sorry about my daughter and husband, but my second husband was so good to me. I am grateful to him for the lifestyle he provided.

Lesson:

Love crosses time and space with soulmates.

Awareness and Connection:

Barbara married the first husband, who reincarnated to complete the unfinished *Karmic* love. The doctor had been the terrorist leader who had been Barbara's second husband. In both lifetimes, Barbara has had a choice.

In this life her husband has provided her with all of the riches and luxury she had with her terrorist husband from the past life. He may have chosen wealth to win her admiration in this life.

He also was able to call in the same soul of the child lost in the past life to be with her again, only this time to complete his caretaking and love. Once again, karmic balance. The doctor is able to care for her and her daughter in this life as their healer, not abuser, healing the wounds from the past.

Relationships

The Indian with the Turban

Abe came to my office complaining about his daughter. Ever since she had been born, Abe had felt a conflict with her, which ended in fights as she got older. They always disagreed about everything and would always fight. Abe got along with his two other children and just could not figure out why he was always so angry with Adrienne and she with him.

We just keep butting heads!

Intention:

Let's go back to the lifetime that brought you into this life with your daughter Adrienne, causing you two to be so angry at each other.

I regressed Abe back to a lifetime where he was an Indian man wearing a turban. His daughter in that life was his daughter Adrienne in this life. They had a sweet life together as child and father, but as Adrienne got older, she developed a mind of her own. At sixteen years old, Adrienne fell in love with a man outside their caste system. Abe was furious, explaining to her why that could not happen and the shame it would bring to the family.

Adrienne would sneak out at night to see her boyfriend, only to be found by her father, who would drag her back to their small house and lock her in her room. Her father put up a fence around the house to keep her safe and inside.

Every week, Adrienne ran away to find her lover, and every week Abe dragged her home and locked her in her room. Adrienne would sob since she wanted to be with her lover and screamed at her father that she hated him for not allowing her to be with him.

Adrienne could not take it anymore, and, during the last lock-in, she hanged herself and died. If she could not be with her lover, she didn't want to live. Abe was angry that she had continually disobeyed him and finally brought shame on the family by hanging herself.

Last Thoughts:

I hate my father and do not want to live if I can't be with my lover.

Lesson:

Respect

Awareness and Connection:

Abe had Adrienne do a past life, too, to see if this could help both of them. Abe's wife was skeptical about past lives and the validity of the work, so she did not want to do one. After I saw both Abe and Adrienne, they decided to wait to share their regressions until they got home so they could tell Abe's wife about what they discovered.

Abe went first, sharing his regression as the Indian man when he noticed his wife's expression of shock. She said, "Abe, don't you remember when Adrienne used to come to our bed when she was three years old with nightmares about the Indian man with a turban who dragged her through the gate?" Adrienne, Abe, and his wife gasped since they all remembered the same image and memory. Little did they know it was actually a past life.

Abe's wife became a believer, and Abe and Adrienne now have a wonderful relationship, understanding where and why they were both so angry at each other. They were able to forgive each other and learned a lesson about respect. They each tried to respect each other from then on.

CHAPTER TWO

Physical Illness and Maladies

Medical research has shown a high incidence of illnesses stemming from emotions. We know stress or fear can cause migraines, ulcers, heart attacks, high blood pressure, etc. This chapter demonstrates that illnesses may have their emotional roots in past lives. The cellular memory in the body holds those negative emotions over lifetimes, causing the manifestation of illnesses in this life.

In Chapter Two, there are stories that exhibit manifestations of illness resulting from past-life times. When the emotions relating to the illness are released, the illness almost always disappears.

Physical Illness

<u>Mangled Legs</u>

Harold came to see me to understand why he had come into this life with cerebral palsy. He explained that his father was an alcoholic and a doctor in this life. When his father found out he had a baby with CP, he became furious.

When Harold was a small boy, his father would beat him because of his disability. When Harold was a teenager, his father would continue to beat him and kick him when he was down.

"God brought me into this world with a physical disability and cursed me with an abusive father surrounding the disability. Did I life-script cerebral palsy?"

Intention:

Let us go back to the life that brought you into this life causing you to have your physical disability.

Harold regressed back to a young boy of eight years of age. I noted that he was shaking in the hypnosis chair. He thought the lifetime he was experiencing was in the early 1800s. He explained that he lived in a log cabin with his mother and father. His father, who is his father in this life, would always drink and come home a nasty drunk. He would become abusive to Harold and his mother, swinging at whomever got in his way. Neither he nor his mother would speak in the house, fearing the father's reprisal. He hated his father.

At this point, Harold started to experience a common phenomenon. He started to shiver, saying that he was very cold. When my clients experience intense fear in the lifetime, they will sometimes become cold.

Harold and his mother lived in constant fear, never knowing when or if the father would be in a mood and strike out.

One day, the father came home drunk and especially abusive. As the father tried to hit Harold, his mother intervened. This enraged the father even more, and he turned and started beating her as well. She fell and hit her head on the corner stone of the fireplace, causing her to become unconscious and bleed. The father then turned back to the boy, threw him on the floor, and started kicking and beating him.

The young boy could not move. His legs were badly broken and mangled. (Harold started rubbing his legs in the hypnosis chair.) His mother's dress caught on fire, and soon the house was covered in flames. Both mother and son died in the fire.

Last Thoughts:

I wish I could help my mother; I can't move.

Lesson:

Independence and strength

Awareness and Connections:

Harold could plainly see why he and his father were back working on this Karma. The father had damaged the boy's legs and turned his back on him after beating him so badly. That is why the father agreed to work on this issue here.

Harold's beaten legs in that life translated into cerebral palsy in this life. His father has not learned his lesson about abuse since he still beat his children in this life. Harold has learned to speak up to his father, telling him what a horrible man he is and telling him he can no longer hurt him since he would leave and never turn back.

Harold is living independently with his disability, sharing a condo with a lovely woman who has taken him in as a roommate. This woman has been very kind to him, treating him as a son. It turns out this woman was his mother in that horrible lifetime.

Harold has fulfilled his lesson here, for he is independent and strong, and he and his new mother can take care of each other without fear. Harold's gait has improved, and, ironically, his new mother's psoriasis (arising from the burnt skin from the fire in that past life) has gotten remarkably better. She sat and listened to the regression and had a healing of her own.

Physical Illness

<u>Watch Out for the Shelling!</u>

Ann came to see me due to her horrific migraine headaches that have prevented her from working.

"I can barely get up some mornings!"

Intention:

Let us go back to the root of your migraine headaches.

I regressed Ann back to a 1950s lifetime. She saw herself in the mirror as a young girl of twelve. She described herself as having a ponytail that she brushed over and over. She sounded perky as she described herself to me. She described her house as a small, yellow home that she thought was in North Carolina. She said she was very close to her family since she was an only child.

I progressed Ann ahead to eighteen years old, where she saw herself interested in nursing. Upon graduation from high school, she and her friends signed up for the army. She wanted to go to nursing school and afterwards to go help the soldiers in Viet Nam.

However, Ann's parents were devastated and admonished her for this decision. She ended up crying. Feeling broken-hearted at her parents' reaction, tears ran down Ann's face. In the hypnosis chair, her frustration showed in her furrowed brow and body movements.

Nevertheless, Ann stuck to her guns and explained to her parents that she had to go. She said, "These poor boys need our help, and I can help. I will be a good nurse." Her parents still tried to talk her out of it, but they knew she was adamant.

They lovingly supported her, and when the day came to go, they brought her to the bus stop.

We progressed to Ann's destination in Viet Nam. She was shown to her housing in a canvas tent.

Ann's first experience was with a wounded soldier who had been severely burned. There was nothing she could do for him except be supporting and hold his hand for comfort. Again, tears streamed down her face as she was shaking. "He's going to die, and I can't help him. He is in a lot of pain." Fear was running through Ann, so we released that emotion.

The soldier died. Feeling helpless and scared, Ann continued to help others. It became so overwhelming that she turned numb. Once again, we released the fear and helplessness.

We progressed to age nineteen, one year later. Ann heard shelling getting close to their hospital. As she ran for safety, she was suddenly hit and died immediately. She saw herself lying face-down on the ground and described the blood coming out of her ear. She assumed she had had some sort of major head trauma.

Last Thoughts:

It's so close; I've got to get to safety before I get it by the shelling.

Lesson:

Live life fully

Awareness and Connections:

Ann could hardly believe that she could have lived during the time of Viet Nam. She realized that the head trauma was partially responsible for her headaches here. She realized why the migraines were so severe. She found that she needed to go into seven more lifetimes to find release for her migraines to go away. For each lifetime in which we released the traumas or negative emotions, the severity of the headaches lessened. Ann was thrilled but never came back for the seventh regression.

Ann was nineteen when she came to see me. We discussed the possibility that her family from the 1950s might still be alive. She was too fearful they would think she was crazy if she let them know she had been reincarnated.

There is a tribute to the nurses who had died during the Viet Nam War. There were not many. At the memorial, I found the name of the nurse Ann had given me. When I researched further, I verified the information Ann described in her session—her address, nursing school, etc.

Physical Illness

<u>Stand in Your Truth</u>

Barbara came to me to see if we could help her arthritis heal.

"I wanted to stay out of their dance."

Intention:

Let us go back to the life that brought you into this life with rheumatoid arthritis.

I regressed Barbara back to a life where she saw herself as a female sitting outside near a small wooden house surrounded by woods. It was a very, very small house. She described her mother as having long, dark hair and noticed that her mother was frail, guarded, and careful. Her father was stern, big, and the boss of the family. She had younger siblings, one of each. Her parents would fight constantly, and the father was abusive. She strove to stay out of their altercations.

When I asked how she felt emotionally, she said, "I feel very separate and on my own. I wanted to stay out of their dance."

When I progressed her to thirteen years old, someone had killed her father. She felt so much freer; she was able to live without having to worry about him anymore. She left her home to go work and lived in a boarding house room. Her only sanctuary was this waterfall outside of town. There, she could think and have quiet moments. She became friendly with the innkeeper, and they would have very long talks.

Eventually, I progressed her to twenty years old, where she saw herself spending more time alone. She became very fearful in terms of marriage. She did not want her marriage to be like that of her parents'. I had Barbara release the fear of her life ending up like her parents'.

She did not have any friends. She lived alone, but she was not lonely. She realized as time went on that she had certain healing capabilities. If she would pray for people, they would seem to get better. If she used her hands, that seemed to help even more. She learned to start using herbs and things of that nature so that she could start to use her healing capabilities.

I then progressed her to twenty-five years old, where she saw herself living in a cabin. People knew she was different from them and knew she could never be married and subservient to a husband. She wanted to be alone. Yet they still came to see her when they needed her help. Some of them called her names, but others realized that whatever she was doing with her healing abilities, it helped people. Using her hands, she felt very blessed, for she would heal mostly children. She was quiet and at peace with herself. Barbara's whole demeanor changed with a relaxed look on her face.

When I progressed her to thirty years old, she saw herself with a scarf around her head as if she was hiding from something and was somewhere she was not supposed to be. Somebody had brought her to royalty to help a member of the royal family, an older man who was in bed, sick and dying. She was helping him move on. That was not what they wanted, but that was all she could do at that time. Angrily, they let her go.

At age thirty-five, we saw her drawing in the dirt with some children, seeing beyond the physical. When she would go to the waterfall, she would listen in a meditative state. She would learn lessons from her guides and her teachers because this was her greatest joy.

At forty years old, just before she passed on, she saw a ring of people in her mind. The night of her death, she actually saw those same people she saw in her mind with torches outside her window and someone coming for her. These were people who did not know what a wonderful healer she was, people who were fearful of her abilities, people who would finally take her life. She was frightened. She knew what was coming, but she did not know where to go or what to do. So she sat quietly.

Barbara was stoned to death by the townspeople. They thought she was evil since she knew how to heal people. They were afraid of her powers.

Before she died, she had a lump in her throat. She wanted to explain, but she knew it would be no use, that there was nothing she could say to save herself from the fear that everybody carried for her.

Last Thoughts:

It will be their loss.

Lesson

Stand in your truth and speak your voice.

Awareness and Connection:

When we asked what that life had to do with her arthritis, she said she had to follow the path that was true to her even if she did not understand it and was never able to express herself. She could not explain these healing powers, and because of her inability to explain them, she admitted it manifested in an arthritic way.

She also held onto shame of being different, since the towns people made her feel badly about herself. Barbara lost her life using her hands for healing. The pain from the stoning remained in her hands in this life as arthritis. We released the pain, the shame, and the trauma. Over time, Barbara's arthritis became less painful.

Barbara also found that her thyroid condition got better since the regression. We had released the energetic block from her throat for not being able to express herself.

This regression also helped Barbara to see why she had been so fearful with regard to her career and fearful of stepping into her full power.

Physical Illness

Torn in Half

Lucy came to see me since she was having problems with her husband sexually. She would dread going to bed with him, for she knew she would have issues with sexual intimacy. She was very bored in their sex life but afraid to speak up about it as not to hurt his feelings. She harbored lots of guilt around it and wasn't sure why.

"I love my husband, but I dread going to bed with him."

Intention:

Let us go back to the lifetime that brought you into this lifetime feeling a sexual disinterest toward your husband.

As we went back, Lucy regressed to a young girl in the 1780s living in a small town in New Hampshire. At ten years old, she saw herself wearing a white pinafore, holding hands with her mother, walking and shopping in a town. She felt the warmth of her father, but her mother seemed to feel very "dizzy" to her. She did go to school at ten years old in a one-room schoolhouse, and she liked school very much. (Lucy was talking like a child when answering my questions.)

I progressed her to fifteen years old. She was running through the grass, playing alone, and was happy. She could feel her height since she was very tall. She saw that she had brown curly hair. She had a boyfriend named Brendan, and she blushed in the hypnosis chair as she described him. He, too, had gone to school, but at fifteen years old, they were no longer in school together. Lucy would help out at home with the chores, and Brendan would come to visit her often.

As I progressed her to twenty years old, she saw herself in her wedding dress marrying Brendan. She was very happy and very pregnant. She ended up having a daughter, and she was very happy about that.

As I progressed her further along to twenty-five years old, she saw herself standing by a fence. She was planting in the garden, and she seemed to be very concerned. There seemed to be some fighting going on with some local Native Americans. One Native American came to visit them often. He befriended both her and her husband. Her child, her little girl, was very shy, but he became a friend to the child as well.

As I progressed her to thirty years old, she saw herself walking on a path in the woods to the stream. She met her Indian friend there, and they became intimate. It was a very passionate relationship. Often, she would go off and meet him. She fell deeply in love with him, yet she felt fearful and guilty because she loved her husband as well. She felt torn.

As I progressed her to thirty-five years old, she was washing clothes by the stream. The Indian was coming to the stream to meet her. He was shot by an arrow and killed.

Lucy sobbed in the hypnosis chair for her lover. This affected her husband as well. She was feeling very depressed. Her daughter, who was very beautiful and kind to her, could not even cheer her up. It was not enough for her. She started losing interest in being with her husband in any passionate kind of way. She would remember how passionate she was with the Indian.

I progressed her further along to forty-five years old, where she was working in the garden, growing her vegetables. It was a hot and dry day, and she was alone and feeling lonely.

Lucy could not find the same joy with her husband, but, finally, she approached him one night. He pretended he was sleeping. He was always in the living room reading or sleeping. He was not meeting her emotional or physical needs since she had pushed him away over the years. He had given up.

As we progressed along, she saw herself at sixty-two years old. She was in bed, and she was dying. Once again, Lucy started sobbing. I asked her why she was crying. She responded, "I can no longer live life without passionate love." Her husband was there. She had a fever and was burning up when finally sweet death took her to her lover.

Last Thoughts:

How much she loved her daughter and how she so missed her Indian lover

Lesson:

Not to be by herself, not to feel isolated or alone

Awareness and Connection:

In this life, Lucy's husband is the same husband she had in her past life. In this lifetime, Lucy's cellular memory of her past husband carries the lack of passion, the passion for which she so longed and remembered from the past life with her Indian lover.

Lucy now understands why she feels dread when she goes to bed with her husband. We discussed what she could do to help bridge the gap or void she feels. We did some soul fragment work to bring back the part of her soul that was "split" or that went with her Indian lover. The integration seemed to help, but Lucy said she would find some new ways to bring the passion back with her husband once again.

Physical Illness

The Screams Gone Unheard

Lisa came to do a regression to find understanding about her irritable bowel syndrome that has made her so unhappy in this life.

"I have such trouble going to the bathroom that I am almost anorexic."

Intention:

Let us go back to the lifetime where Lisa's bowel issues began so we can release the emotion or trauma that created this terrible bowel syndrome.

The story unfolds with Lisa going back to the warm, rolling hills of Kentucky in the late 1800s. She saw herself living in a small house but also having all the amenities of wealth around her. She was three years old and saw herself in a big, fluffy bed with her mother and father standing over her, telling her that she was a bad girl.

Lisa began crying in the hypnosis chair as she was feeling great embarrassment. She was not sure why she was a bad girl until she finally got a chance to see her parents' black servant washing her down, removing her own excrement from her hair and her body. Lisa had not only soiled herself but also had it all over her body. She was being reprimanded for it.

Lisa then continued forward to ten years old. She was crying and sad because she felt very lonely. I helped Lisa release the sadness and loneliness. I could see the disgust for herself on her face. She even said under her breath, "This is so disgusting."

Lisa remembered her parents going on a trip, leaving her with their servants to care for her. A black man, Smitty, was fond of Lisa and seemed to be her primary caregiver. He would feed her and wash her down. She smiled as she spoke of him.

Lisa gasped at the realization that she appeared to be autistic, not able to understand much of anything other than the simple pleasures of using her senses.

As we progressed forward, Lisa saw herself at age fifteen putting her excrement all over her body, feeling good from the sensation. Again, Lisa winced at the thought of what the autistic girl was doing.

Being autistic, Lisa's only way of communication or feeling was through her excrement, being able to rub it on her body, and letting Smitty wash it off with the gentle water. It felt good to her. It felt soft and soothing.

But everyone made Lisa feel ashamed of what she had done. She knew there was something wrong with it, but she did not care as it felt so good.

As Lisa progressed through her life, Smitty was the only person who stayed to take care of her. Her parents never returned, for it was too hard for them. So they sent Smitty money for her care. He loved her deeply in his heart, maybe because he felt sorry for her and identified with her shame. Maybe because he knew that everyone had abandoned Lisa.

After many years, when Lisa reached twenty years old, Smitty would come only every six months or so to make sure that there was food and that she was alive. He taught her how to clean herself, which she liked to do, but she still continued to rub excrement on her body.

She did not feel lonely when all those who abandoned her left; she only felt lonely when they came. It was then that she realized what she was missing while they were there with her. In particular, Smitty's visits made her very sad as she missed him so. She would get agitated when he came.

Every day, she continued in her rituals, sitting in a corner, putting her excrement all over her body, and then cleaning herself.

By the time Lisa was twenty-five, Smitty had passed on, and a new black man came to be her new caretaker. This new black man ended up raping Lisa in that lifetime.

Lisa curled up in the hypnosis chair as she reported the rape. She was so fearful. She did not understand. Once again, she retreated into the place of using her excrement to make herself feel better.

Once again, I helped Lisa release the fear attached to the rape.

When she was terrified and certainly in pain, the man would then callously hose her down. Again, more releasing. Lisa was sobbing.

When Lisa reached twenty-eight years old, this man not only came to rape Lisa but also to beat her to death. He could not stand watching her put the excrement over her body anymore. Lisa died in that rape and beating. The horrific screams went unheard.

Last Thoughts:

I'm disgusting; I should have run away.

Lesson:

Compassion for self

Awareness and Connection:

In this lifetime, Lisa's lesson is to take care of herself at a soul level and to make sure she stands up for herself here. Certainly, the connection for Lisa in that lifetime was about her bowel movements and how they made her feel good. But because of her autism and bowel movements, she was taken advantage of, shamed by everyone around her, raped, and killed.

For Lisa in this lifetime, fear of impending death manifested in these intestinal/bowel problems. Lisa has had terrible problems with eating issues, causing her to be terribly thin. She had done all kind of work on this already but with no resolution. The eating issues were also a result of the fear around bowel movements. If she ate, it would result in a bowel movement.

We released the fear that was attached to her shame, rape, and death stemming from what she had done to herself in that lifetime. Now, Lisa could come forward in this present lifetime, no longer in fear of her bowel movements and with an understanding from where this fear came. Lisa had three more lifetimes to go through to completely clear her fear of having a bowel movement.

This history also provided an understanding of some aspects of the psychological make-up of an autistic child. Lisa is a psychotherapist in this life. Perhaps she can use this regression to help parents understand more about their autistic children.

Physical Illness

Watch Where You Are Going

Sam's mother had done past-life therapy work with me and had great success. Since Sam had ADD, his mom asked if her son would benefit from such treatment, too. I had never worked with a child of eleven with such a diagnosis before. However, this work has healed multiple-personality disorders, so I felt compelled to try. We decided to let Sam request what he felt he needed in forming our intention. Sam said, "I want to find out where my focus problem is coming from." That became our intention.

"I have ADD and want to know why I cannot focus."

Intention:

Let us go back to the root of your focus problem.

I regressed Sam back to a lifetime in the year 1931. He was a twelve-year-old boy living in the city of Boston. He gave me great details of names, addresses, schools, etc. He said his name was Bob. He saw himself outside playing stickball with his friend Frank. He described his house as a blockhouse with a fence around it. When asked where his mother was, he said she was in the house doing housework. He noted that his mother in his past life was his father in this life.

Bob enjoyed playing basketball and became really good. He and his friends would play next to the school. He described a gang of boys who would taunt him and his friends while they played.

As we progressed to eighteen years of age, Bob saw himself in the comic store. When asked if he still went to school, he replied,

"No, I play basketball for the Knicks." I assumed he meant pro basketball.

When I asked if he had a girlfriend, he responded with a smile on his face, "Yes. She works in the grocery store. She has brown hair and blue eyes. I'm going to marry her." When I asked if he did marry her, he said yes and that she was his sister in this life. His smile turned into a frown of disgust. "Eww, my sister!"

When I progressed him to twenty years old, he informed me that he had a baby boy. They had moved to New York City in an apartment. He saw himself watching television while Mary, his wife, was in the kitchen cooking.

We then progressed to thirty-five years old, where he saw himself drive his first car, a sports car. He said he started playing baseball for the Yankees. He said he had a best friend on the team named Steve.

I wondered about playing two different sports, both on professional teams. However, he gave me many details to corroborate his story.

At age fifty, Bob's wife, Mary, died of a heart attack. Bob started to cry in the hypnosis chair. He really was sad that his wife had died. I helped him release the sadness through breath work.

As we progressed to age sixty, Bob said, "I came up the stairs after shopping and put the groceries on the kitchen table. As I turn to go down the stairs, I fell down those stairs, and those stairs, and those stairs." I assume he meant three flights of stairs. Bob continued, "I broke all the bones in my body. They took me off to the hospital, and I died there." Bob was very matter-of-fact reporting the story to me.

Last Thoughts:

I miss Mary. If I focused and watched where I was going, I would not have fallen and died.

Lesson:

Safety

Awareness and Connection:

Bob was so excited that he understood where his ADD came from and that it was not because he is stupid. It is just to remind him to watch where he is going.

After releasing all of the negative emotions, Bob started to make more eye contact with the adults around him. He seemed to have more patience and tolerance for others. Bob is not cured, but he is in a state of transformation. He is learning all he has come here to learn.

Bob's story did not exactly jibe with some of the information we checked; however, the acknowledgement, the releasing, and the story had impact on his healing.

Physical Illness

<u>Migraines</u>

Casey came to me presenting with symptoms of severe migraine headaches. During a history intake, she informed me that since her baby had been born three months earlier, she had been getting seventeen migraines a week. When asked when she remembered getting the first migraine in this life, she recounted it happening at the onset of her first menstruation. However, she would only get them once a month and only one day of her period.

Casey told me she had been to many doctors, especially neurologists, to seek their help. They found nothing organically wrong with her and only offered painkillers. She felt that they didn't help and that she could not function in this pain with her new baby. When a headache would come on, she would have to go to bed with blinds shut and the room darkened. Often she would vomit due to the pain. She said this situation made her feel "trapped."

I received additional history about her family, her husband, and the childbirth, none of which sounded suspicious regarding the headaches.

"I want to be with my baby!"

Intention:

Let's go back to the root of your migraine headaches.

When under, Casey went into a past lifetime around the early 1800s. She saw herself living in a small house in the country, on a farm. When asked to look back over the first thirteen years of her life to see if anything significant happened, she contracted and started crying. She said her father had raped her a few years after her mother passed away. She became pregnant, feeling "trapped" and ashamed. She stayed at home most of the time doing chores and disassociating to cope. Through breath work and visualization, I had her release the feeling of being "trapped" and the deep shame she carried. She was thirteen years old when this happened.

As I progressed her further, she saw herself walking in town pregnant. Feeling out of her body, she got hit by a horse and wagon and hit her head on the cobblestone street, where she died. Death came so fast she had no time to think of anything before she died. However, she died carrying the shame of being pregnant and of what happened to her.

Last Thoughts:

None (It happened too fast.)

Lesson:

Forgiveness

Awareness and Connection:

I asked how that life affected her migraines in this life.

We were told that the rape, pregnancy, and death were all tied together. The head trauma at death resulted as she carried the trauma of conception. This explained why she presented with headaches both at menstruation and after childbirth. The body's cellular memory was triggered by her connection to her age and the conception of her baby. Conception and head trauma once again revisited.

Casey called several months after our session to inform me that her migraines had disappeared but that she occasionally still gets headaches.

When I asked her how many lifetimes she needed to release from to clear the headaches, we were told three more.

Casey can now function as a mother and wife without feeling "trapped" or in severe pain. She will be coming to me to do the other three lifetimes so we can clear all of her headaches.

My client's doctors are amazed that she no longer suffers from her migraines.

Physical Illness

Responsibilities

Becky was a bit skeptical about Past Life Regressions. She came with an attitude of "prove it to me; I really don't believe in past lives." Yet she said she was hoping that it would be real since she really wanted to get rid of her asthma. Becky was a news reporter who brought her cameraman to tape our session. Later, I was grateful for the camera's witness.

"Please get rid of my asthma!"

Intention:

Let us go back to the root of your asthma.

I regressed Becky back to a farm life in the 1800s. She saw herself as a young girl of twelve helping her mother cook in the kitchen. As we went back to ten years old to see her with the rest of her family, we saw her feeding the chickens with her father. In both cases, we saw very little interaction with either parent. Her emotional state was somewhat flat.

I then progressed Becky to age fifteen, where she saw herself sweeping the floors in the farmhouse. Her mother was cooking, so once again there was very little interaction. She was an only child, so her exposure to other people was limited.

We then progressed to age twenty, where we saw that Becky had married and was sewing. Her relationship with her husband was not emotional but more practical. However, she seemed content. Her parents were not that far away, so Becky got to visit them often. Again, she saw herself with her mother hanging up the laundry.

We progressed to age twenty-five, where we saw Becky now with a child, again cooking. When asked if she liked having a baby, she responded, "It's okay." I asked her how her relationship with her husband was, and she said the same thing, "It's okay."

As we progressed to age thirty, Becky started to notice that she was not so happy and quite bored with her life. Becky even displayed bored movements in the hypnosis chair. However, she realized that she had responsibilities, and this would be her life forever. Becky felt trapped but acquiescent.

We progressed to age thirty-five and found things were still the same. Becky was raising their child, cooking, cleaning, doing farm chores, etc. She had little interaction with her husband, and what they did have was more like a business partnership. He took care of the farm, and she took care of the house.

At age forty, Becky was milking the cows. She noticed that she had some abdominal distress. She was actually clutching her abdomen in the chair. Becky continued to get worse, having great pain, a fever, and vomiting. Due to the needs of the farm, Becky's husband was unable to stay with her to help her through her illness. Becky's son was there putting cool cloths on her forehead. Becky died from (we think) appendicitis.

Last Thoughts:

I was smothered by responsibilities.

Lesson:

Duty: I was a dutiful child, dutiful wife, and a dutiful mother.

Awareness and Connection:

Becky's last thought in her past life manifested into a physical condition in her present one. Perhaps she needed it to remember that life is more than hard work and complacency. Becky was lacking love and joy in her life, feeling it was her duty to live without them. Becky connected her present asthma to those thoughts, even though she felt she had made it all up. I assured

Becky that she need not feel smothered by responsibilities anymore. She could enjoy her responsibilities as long as she created pleasure in her life. I also told her that she no longer needed her asthma—that, if she chose to, she could let it go.

Becky came out of the session still questioning the validity of her experience. She felt she had made it all up. During the session, Becky's pager had gone off. She opened her eyes and asked if she could answer it. I said yes but that we would pick up where we left off when she came back. She rubbed her eyes, repeating, "I think I made up the whole thing. I also don't think I was under hypnosis." I reassured her that we would analyze the whole experience. When she decided that she did not need to answer the page, she again repeated that she did not feel that she had been under. Reluctantly, she came back and sat down. I told her that at the count of three, she could go right back to the place we had left off. She went under immediately and picked up where we had left off. Even the cameraman did a double-take since she went under so quickly—especially since she felt she had not been under at all.

Later, when she questioned her experience, the cameraman told her it was real. Becky may not ever believe in it; however, she has the awareness of from where her asthma might have come. If she does not believe it, she may hamper the healing process.

This regression shows the power of our last thoughts. Even a metaphor (versus an act) can manifest physically.

We have to be open to healing and want to heal most of the time for it to happen. If she were truly interested in healing, even if she did not believe in past lives, the healing would still occur. When Becky left, she had more intent to prove me wrong than to heal. It still might have happened, for her subconscious might have wanted the healing badly enough to surpass her ego. She never called again, so I do not know the ending or what the final results were; however, I was told that her asthma had healed.

CHAPTER THREE

Unworthiness

Sometimes we become self-destructive by disregarding our health, abusing drugs and alcohol, neglecting self-nurturing, sleep, work, relationships, or by our choice of career paths. These self-destructive patterns come from our past in this life and from past lives. They are unworthy remnants from negative emotions such as guilt, shame, anger, revenge, sadness, and fear. Our subconscious or cellular memory holds on to these remnants, creating self-destructive patterns. Subconsciously, we do not feel worthy of anything good in our lives. We hold on to old tapes that say, "I don't deserve…"

Unworthiness

Please Like Me

Sandy came to see me since she was tired of everyone taking advantage of her and that she would allow them to do so. She would get so angry at herself that she would not say *no* more often. She said she never wanted to hurt anyone's feelings and always wanted everyone to like her.

"I hurt myself to avoid hurting others."

Intention:

Let us go back to the root of your feelings of unworthiness.

I regressed Sandy back to a lifetime in 1941. She saw herself as a young woman sitting by a pond with her husband, happy and in love. She described that the pond was on their apple tree farm in Rhode Island. Sandy recognized the husband as her son in this life.

Sandy went into the house to cook dinner for her husband and herself. While she was frying their dinner, Sandy went to the bathroom and returned to a smoke-filled kitchen. The curtains had caught on fire, filling the whole house with smoke. Sandy passed out, only to awaken in the hospital. She had survived, but her husband had died in the fire.

Sandy cried at the thought that she had killed her husband and said, "We never even had children." Sandy's husband comes into this life as her child. In her past life, Sandy tried to start a new life out in California, seeking to get over her tragic accident. She met another man who was very social and married him only to find out that he had cheated on her and was never home.

Still filled with self-blame about her first husband, she finally broke out of reality. Feeling depressed and remorseful, she walked down to and into the Pacific Ocean to end her pain.

Lesson:

Strength

Last Thoughts:

Where are all of my support systems?

Connection and Awareness:

Sandy was very sad that she had killed her first husband in her past life, who is now her son in this life. She felt it made so much sense since she was always trying to please him and dote on him. Sandy was still carrying her guilt from the accident and feeling that she did not deserve to have joy in this life.

Always trying to please everyone else was a way of trying to win back love that she did not get from the second husband. It also helped Sandy understand why she has had trust issues in this life with her present husband. Sandy's cellular memory was still holding that her last husband cheated on her. When we feel that we do not deserve to have joy in this life, we put that energy out there and manifest things and people in our life that will fulfill that prophesy.

Sandy has been looking for those support systems here, but, instead, she attracts those who want her support. After the regression, Sandy understands the reason she has been trying to please everyone, especially her son. After releasing the energy of the guilt, she no longer feels the need to please.

Sandy now has a very healthy relationship with her son and with her family, speaking up and asking for their support when she needs it. A new respect for her has developed within her family.

Unworthiness

Depression

Judy came to see me a bit skeptical about past-life work. She had been suffering since she was three years old with chronic depression, and she thought that just maybe it could be past-life-related. Her mother had been her nemesis her whole life, always telling her she was never "good enough." She also believed her mother, feeling unworthy of anything good happening to her in her life.

"Could Past Life Regression really help me?"

Intention:

Let us go back to the root of your depression.

I regressed Judy back to a medieval lifetime, where she was a man out hunting for his family's survival. He loved his family very much and only wanted to make sure of their happiness. Judy felt her wife in that life was her mother in this one.

As we progressed, he was out hunting again, having great success bringing home the animals for their dinner. When he arrived home, he found his wife and children killed and all that they owned stolen.

This man was so devastated to find his precious family killed that he went into a stupor, wandering around the forest, eating berries, and sleeping under bushes for months until he finally died. His thoughts for those months were that he never should have left, for he was not there to protect his family when they really needed him.

Last Thoughts:

It should have been me instead of them. I do not deserve to live.

Lesson:

Worthiness

Awareness and Connection:

Judy came into this life still feeling depressed from that life about not saving her family. She carried such guilt, self-loathing, and shame that she was not there to protect her family that she did not feel worthy to live here as well. This feeling of self-loathing and desire not to want to live in this life always plagued Judy — not understanding why she felt this way until our regression.

Judy's mother was so upset and angry from her previous life — and that her husband had not been present to protect her while she watched the invaders kill her children and then her — that she came into this life still angry at Judy. Her verbal abuse of Judy compounded Judy's self-loathing so that she continued to carry her depression and low self-worth forward in this life.

Judy finally understood why she had felt this way all these years and why her mother also felt this way. We were able to release the emotions that caused this depression, helping Judy to start her healing process.

Judy had ten more lifetimes from which to release in order to clear her depression completely. Judy reported that she was already feeling better with each regression. Not only did we release the emotional blocks, but she could finally put understanding around her question of "why?"

Unworthiness

Gloria

Upset over her recent divorce and custody battle, in which her children expressed their desire to live with their father, Deborah, age thirty-seven, came to see me extremely upset.

Deborah was torn between fighting for custody of her children and wondering whether they should live with their father since she has a new, live-in boyfriend and wants that relationship to work. Although her boyfriend said that he would be supportive of whatever she wishes to do with regard to her children, she sensed that he would be happier without them.

"Why do I feel so indecisive about making the right choice about my children or fighting for them?" She did not know if she really deserved them or whether her ex-husband did.

"I love my children, but I love my new boyfriend."

Intention:

Let us go back to the lifetime that brought Deborah into this life to see her Karma with her husband and how it may have created the current situation.

We went back to a life in Italy. As a young woman growing up in a very strict family, everything in her life was about work and helping out in the home. All she wanted to do was get married and leave home.

When she was fifteen, she met a man much older than she. She did not love him but married him to escape her family environment. He turned out to be tyrannical and abusive. She cleaned, cooked, and did everything required of her. Her only outlet was visiting her friends, but she was afraid to tell the secret of her husband's abuse to them. They did not suspect because she covered her unhappiness with her charming behavior.

Although she was unhappy with her husband, when she gave birth to a child, she delighted in taking care of her baby. Her baby was also a joy. In her past life, she was a caring, loving, and devoted mother who tried to be a good wife. These children were also her children in this lifetime.

Her husband's abuse and tyranny became worse, and she was beaten up so badly at one point that she left her husband and went off with her children to stay with friends.

Frightened about what her husband had done to her, her friends told her she must hide. She fled in the middle of the night and took her children to an island.

After her disappearance, her husband searched, questioning everyone as to her whereabouts. Frightening one of her friends into disclosing where she had gone, he went to bring her and the children back.

He found them, beat her once again, and then dragged them back home, threatening to kill her if she tried to leave. Feeling lost and helpless, she was so frightened and weak that she stayed, allowing the beatings.

She fed him, clothed him, and did her wifely duties as well as her motherly duties. Defeated, she sank into a deep depression. She knew she needed to escape but feared for her children's safety. So she left without her children.

Once again, her husband came looking for her and found her. This time, he beat her to death.

Last Thoughts:

I can't do it anymore. I don't have the strength. I just want to leave. Although she had guilt and sadness about leaving her children, she felt helpless. There was nothing she could do to protect them or herself any longer.

Lesson:

To be strong—she has been unable to fulfill that because she had been beaten down so many times.

Awareness and Connection:

Her lesson here was about speaking her voice.

In the custody battle, she realized that if she wanted her children, she had to fight for them, which she had not done in her past life. This time, she has to speak up and speak her truth about what she wants regardless of whether her new boyfriend or her ex-husband disagrees. At this point in time, this is her role.

Now that we have removed the energy that prevented her from speaking her voice and have given her the understanding of her role through the connection to her past life, she can be decisive, strong, and understand why she felt unworthy to have her children. Hopefully, the custody battle will go in her favor. We do not know at this time.

Note:

All of the above people felt unworthy in their intention. In the last case, the mother felt unworthy to take her children and carried that feeling of unworthiness from that lifetime where she did not feel she fought hard enough for her children.

In all the other cases, people carried unworthy feelings such as not deserving to have the job, the relationship, the health, the self-care, and self-love due to the baggage they carried from those past lives.

Unworthiness

The Family Caretaker

Victoria came in feeling depressed about being a caretaker for her family and not having time and energy to fulfill her goals.

"Why doesn't anyone ever think to take care of me?"

Intention:

Let us go back to the lifetime that makes it difficult for you to step into your full power in this life.

Victoria regressed back into her past lifetime as a teenager living in a stone house in the plains of America. I regressed her back to the age of ten, where she was happily sitting with her family at a picnic table. She had two loving parents and siblings with her at the table in a vegetable garden. At fourteen years old, she had had to bury her younger brother, who had drowned.

At sixteen years old, she moved to the city so she could make money for herself and her family. She became a servant to a stern, wealthy family who lived in a large town house. She worked there unhappily for many more years until she finally returned home at age twenty-eight to an empty house. Her family had moved or died.

At age forty-three, she fell ill with tuberculosis and could not breathe. She never married nor had a family of her own. So the only one by her deathbed was a nun.

Last Thoughts:

I am not very happy. I am glad to go. I should have stayed with my own family.

Lesson:

Unworthiness/devotion

Victoria had led a life void of many real, fulfilling relationships with people other than her family. She had cherished her family but had left for financial reasons. When she finally came home, there was no one there—leaving her with only memories. Victoria had learned devotion and came here with a new lesson: how to balance devotion to others and still take care of herself and her family.

Awareness and Connection:

Victoria seemed to be able to find the balance she needed to complete her lesson. Now that she released the fears she held in her cellular memories, she learned how to set boundaries with her family and friends, be devoted, and yet ask for her needs to be met and for their support.

Unworthiness

Success

Andy came in feeling frustrated because he was not achieving financial success, nor was he doing what he loved to do.

"I can't seem to keep a dollar."

Intention:

To go back to the lifetime that now prevents you from receiving abundance in this life.

Andy regressed to being a young boy. In this previous lifetime, he saw his dad (also his dad in this life) as a prominent banker with many enemies. He felt constantly stressed because he feared that bad things would happen to his father and his financial achievements. At twenty years old, he felt obligated to help his father with banking, even though his passion was writing.

At thirty years old, Andy was in a position of authority, and many people consulted with him about political matters. He enjoyed the role more than banking. Andy had a wife, although he spent most of his time in town with his fellow men.

Later, Andy's fears heightened when his brother died in a manner related to his family's great fortune. He resented his family's money because it had only brought trouble.

At forty years old and constantly fearing assassination, Andy pulled away from his family's business to become a writer. He wrote and used his artistic creativity to escape worry.

At forty-five, Andy saw himself on his deathbed after having been poisoned. There was no escaping his family's businesses and reputation.

Last Thoughts:

I would have done more as a writer. I helped plenty of people, and the one time I let my guard down, I was poisoned.

Lesson:

Worthiness/trust

Awareness and Connection:

Andy's cellular memories were that money and pursuit of his passion brought death and disaster, and these memories prevented him from achieving abundance in this life.

As a banker, Andy had been cautiously protective of his money. When Andy began to immerse himself in writing, he was so wrapped up in his joy that he lost the awareness that he still needed to protect his family and finances. The result of letting down his guard was to be poisoned.

We released the energy attached to these fears concerning the consequences of money and doing what he loved. He was then able to move forward, pursuing the writing without the fear of it causing his demise. Further, he did not have to worry about his investments and their future earnings, since the investments were protected by banking regulations and experts not related to him.

Unworthiness

Abundance

Janet came into my office feeling she had not achieved abundance in love, finance, or career. She wanted to see what might be blocking her from achieving what she desired and deserved.

"What is blocking me from receiving abundance in my life?"

Intention:

Let's go to the root of what is blocking you from receiving abundance in this life.

Janet regressed to a lifetime as a monk, where she had made vows of poverty, chastity, and obedience. (Until fulfilled or cleared, vows are one of the most powerful energies that can block someone from achieving whatever violates those vows.)

In that regression, she saw herself as a young boy living in England. There, his parents barely had enough to feed the family. At fifteen, he was sent to the monastery to help the monks and to train for entry into their order.

When he turned twenty years old, he was happy being a part of the monastery. He was content and continued to honor his vows of poverty, chastity, and obedience. The rest of his life was peaceful and quiet.

At the end of his life, he died wondering why he had to die alone. In this life of devotion and sacrifice, no one was around when he needed them.

Last Thoughts:

Where is everybody when I need them after giving my life to poverty, chastity, and obedience?

Lesson:

Commitment

Awareness and Connection:

Even though he fulfilled his obligations, the monk was unable to engage in relationships, leaving him feeling empty and alone.

I asked Janet how many lifetimes she needed to release and clear those vows that blocked her from achieving abundance. She was extremely upset because there were seventeen past lives in which she had been a monk taking those same vows.

After releasing five lifetimes, Janet's practice began flourishing, and her financial abundance started to flow. In addition, she is now involved in a new relationship. She is now receiving her abundance even though we still have many lifetimes to heal. However, until all the lifetimes are cleared, there can still be some resistance due to remnant energy from the lifetimes still not worked on.

Another benefit from this work is that she now feels worthy enough to receive.

After a previous lifetime when Janet had lived in poverty both at home and later in the monastery (where she also had minimal contact with others), Janet now understands why love and money are so important to her. Although she loved the monastic life, after sacrificing so much and feeling alone in the end, she questioned its worth. In this life, she realized why career is so important; however, relationships are more meaningful above all.

Unworthiness

Loser

A thirty-eight-year-old male came to my office to try to understand why he felt like such a "loser." His family never seemed to have much faith in him succeeding in any endeavor. Nothing ever seemed to go right for him. Now, his family looked down on him because he could not seem to hold down a job.

"You are such a loser."

Intention:

Let us go back to the root of your feelings of unworthiness in this life that is preventing you from getting the job you desire and becoming successful.

Steven went back to a lifetime in the late 1700s in Ireland, where he was growing up in poverty. Most of the time, his parents could barely feed their children. They ate only potatoes and whatever roots they could dig up.

Overwhelmed from the number of children they had to feed, his parents were constantly telling him to go hunting or find a job so that they could eat better. In that lifetime, Steven kept looking for a job but found none available due to the great poverty in Ireland.

Finally at fifteen, he decided to run away from the oppression in his family and his country. He became a sailor.

The work was grueling, his earnings were meager, and he was barely able to sustain himself. He wanted to send his earnings to his family, but he never earned enough to do so.

At twenty and frequenting bars, he finally met a woman who also came from the same background of poverty. Lust, not love, brought them together, however. Later, she told him that he was not a good provider and not even good in bed. But he did not leave her.

At twenty-five, he was still working as a sailor and was still unmarried. Feeling bad about himself, he went from bar to bar, getting into drunken stupors.

In continuing correspondence with his family, he received a note from his father stating, "You never amounted to anything and never will." There was a constant barrage of criticism from both his father and girlfriend.

At thirty, he was coerced into marrying the woman with whom he had been in a relationship for many years. Spending more time with her and her shrewish yelling and complaining about the lack of money drove him to take long boat trips to escape the noise. While at sea, the ship sank, and he drowned.

Last Thoughts:

It was all such a waste of time and life. I couldn't support my family. I could barely eat. What was all that about? Why did I need to have a life like that? I'm ready to go.

Lesson:

Self-love

Awareness and Connection:

Steven had patience and perseverance as he kept trying to pursue a better way of life. However, he chose people who were mentally and emotionally abusive; his lesson was about self-love and worthiness. Never amounting to anything according to others, he died with great shame and guilt. His poor choices in relationships in that lifetime brought him into this life with one of the hardest lessons to learn: self-love, yet again.

Having experienced similar drama in this life, in which his parents brought him up in poverty and demanded he work at an early age, Steven understood the connections to this past life.

And in this life, all his relationships ended with someone telling him he was not good enough and he would never make it.

The negative energy that he carried forward prevented him from getting the job he deserved. We removed the energy that had blocked Steven since that lifetime, removing thoughts of guilt and shame. We discussed how he could integrate this information into his life to make better choices in relationships and jobs and how he needed to work on loving himself.

A few months later, Steven returned to clear more lifetimes. The shift became evident when Steven found a well-paying job.

Since the removal of the energy of unworthiness that Steven carried from various lifetimes, we are hopeful that he will be able to move ahead more clearly, loving himself enough to get everything in life he desires.

Unworthiness

Suzanne

Suzanne, a forty-seven-year-old woman, came to see me regarding her healing practice. She had known for a long time that she should be an energy healer. Although she has wanted to do so, something has been blocking her. This has caused her to question whether she is capable of being an energy healer and whether healing work is really what she is meant to do. Despite everyone concurring that she is a gifted healer, she did not trust herself.

"You really are a gifted healer!"

Intention:

Let us go to the root of whatever is blocking you from moving into your full purpose in this lifetime.

I regressed Suzanne to a lifetime in Germany, where she lived in poverty as a young boy named Peter. His unwed mother put him in a basket, leaving it on a road where some young children found it. They brought the basket to a local nunnery that also functioned as an orphanage.

Peter's biological father was married, and his wife had just given birth to a girl. Wanting a male heir and hearing rumors about his mistress's illegitimate son, he began a search for Peter.

By age ten, Peter's father discovered his son's whereabouts and brought him home to be raised as his heir. Peter loved living in luxury, being given clothes, food, and all the things he had missed in his earlier years.

We went forward to fifteen, where Peter was well-dressed and happy helping his father in his business.

At twenty, Peter realized that his father had accumulated his wealth by overworking his employees and paying them meager wages. Because of his own impoverished history, Peter could not tolerate his father's lack of integrity. So he left home to work as a carpenter, a craft he had learned in the orphanage. Peter was taught how to work, whittle, and build with wood.

At twenty-five, Peter met and married a young woman, and they had a baby. Coming from a home with emotionally unavailable parents, his wife was unable to experience any emotions of her own, including love. Peter returned to his father's home with his wife and child, realizing that it would allow him to give his child the benefits his father had given him, including love. Peter decided it was more important to give his child love and family roots than to cling to his anger over his father's business ethics.

His father died when Peter was thirty. By then, Peter was traveling to Asia and Spain in order to build the family businesses, often leaving his wife and child.

At forty, when a war broke out, the government recognized Peter's power and asked him to lead a brigade. Faced with the decision as to whether he wanted to give up his personal power in business or to help the common people in the war, Peter decided to go to war. In the end, he was stabbed on the battlefield.

Last Thoughts:

This was a wasted life. Why does everything have to be about power, control, and money? Why cannot there be peace and a more peaceful existence?

Lesson:

Patience and power — in this lifetime, his lesson is trust, self-forgiveness, and self-love.

Awareness and Connection:

In spite of the fact that Peter did not like his father's ethics, Peter realized the value of providing a good life for his family. So he compromised his values and took over his father's business.

His business responsibilities caused him to travel, separating him from his family. When called to fight, he feared that if he stayed with his family attending to his business, he would not be able to protect them. Yet, if he went to war, he could finance a strong army with his money and strong leadership, which would protect them better than if he stayed at home.

In the end, his choice to go to war took him from his family and resulted in his death, so his efforts to help his country were in vain.

After the regression, Suzanne was able to understand the source of her confusion and resistance, fearing that stepping into full power would result in the loss of family, power, and purpose. Clearing the energy block of fear in the lifetime, Suzanne felt she was free to move forward, knowing she would make the right choices. She was no longer fearful about stepping into her power as a successful healer.

CHAPTER FOUR

Fears and Phobias

Sometimes, we know from where a fear or phobia might be coming. We know when something in this life triggered the fear or phobia, such as witnessing a plane crash and then being terrified to fly again. However, most of us have many fears or phobias that we cannot explain. For example, we may fear heights, water, fire, flying, animals, insects, snakes, or crossing bridges. Most always, we find the root of these fears to be past-life-related.

The stories in this chapter will bring the reader to the root causes of fears and phobias, to see from where they come and why. Then, demonstrating how to release the fear attached to the particular trauma in the story, the fear or phobia is cleared for life.

Fears and Phobias

<u>Snakes!</u>

Laurie came to see me with a horrific fear of snakes. She had just taken her daughter's Brownie group on a camp-out and came back traumatized.

While preparing their tents, a snake had squirmed out and slithered away. Laurie not only had screamed uncontrollably, but she had broken out into a sweat, shaking for a good half-hour. The young Brownies had had to calm her down, although they thought the snake was kind of cool.

Since there would be more camp-outs, Laurie wanted to eliminate this fear so she could be the grown-up next time. When asked if she had ever been bitten by a snake or had had any encounter with one, she said not to her recollection.

"Get me out of here!"

Intention:

Let us go back to the root of your fear of snakes.

I regressed Laurie back to the root of her snake fears or phobia. Laurie ended up in India as a beautiful Indian girl named Wasilla, who lived in a palace. She lived with her mother, who was a caretaker of the prince.

Wasilla was brought up in the confines of the palace and treated very well. The prince treated her like his own sister. She was dressed nicely, fed well, and even taught to read.

As Wasilla grew up, she fell in love with a servant boy. Due to the caste system, they knew they could never be together in the palace. So they planned to run away and live in a village happily ever after.

When they left the palace, the commoners grabbed at them, touching their clothes and hair since they were dressed so nicely. Wasilla was almost mauled until they finally were able to flee into the woods. They enjoyed being in the woods, finally alone and in love.

That evening, Wasilla was bitten by a snake and struck with a terrible fever. The venom was poisonous. She died three days later from the bite.

Last Thoughts:

I should have never left the palace. The woods are an evil place.

Lesson:

Discipline

Awareness and Connection:

Laurie immediately understood from where her fear of snakes came. She also connected with the feeling of leaving the safety of her home. Laurie was always a home body who never wanted to travel or go very far from home. This helped her to finally understand why. Her subconscious fear was if she were to travel away from her home, she would die or be mauled.

It is always prudent to be cautious about snakes since one cannot always know if they are poisonous or not. Now, Laurie will not have such a traumatic response when she sees one but a normal, more centered reaction.

Laurie also laughed and made a positive connection. She always loved fine clothes and jewelry.

Fears and Phobias

<u>Driving</u>

Sixty-five-year-old Sam came to me to help him work on his fear of driving. Part of his fear was his concern about getting lost. He would get lost even when driving in his neighborhood. His heart would race as he approached his car. Sam also had a difficult time sitting in my hypnosis chair. He reported he had rheumatoid arthritis in his hands, knees, and ankles.

"I feel like a goof when I get lost driving anywhere."

Intention:

Let us go to the root of your driving phobia.

During regression, Sam went to eighteen different lifetimes, jumping from one to the next. Each life was revealed using symbols such as numbers, colors, and religious characters. In one of the lifetimes, everything from the color of the sky to his clothing was blue. I had not realized the symbolism until he commented, "There's that blue again." The repetitiveness also happened with numbers.

When Sam finally moved ahead into this life, he saw himself hiding beneath his kitchen table with his father admonishing him for being "a big, stupid goof."

Sam's father seemed to lack emotional understanding. As he watched his son cry in pain from a cut on his finger, Sam's unsympathetic father told him, it's "just a cut. Be tougher." As Sam recalled this incident, he cried.

We released the shame and fear using breath work. By the time we finished, Sam was exhausted. Even though he "cried like a baby," Sam told me he was grateful for the session.

In the next session, Sam returned to his childhood in this life. This time, Sam's father embarrassed him in front of his friends as the boy played stickball on the street, calling him "a goof." At the same moment, Sam witnessed his friend being run over by a trolley. Horrified, Sam cried. Sam's father yelled that Sam should be stronger.

Sitting in my chair, Sam cried while retelling this story. Again, we released the fear and horror of both the witnessed accident and his father's cruel comments. Sam left the office as exhausted as he had been after his previous session. By the end of the year, we released all the shame and fear of this life from his father, teachers, and bosses.

Every week, as Sam became braver, he drove greater distances. After visiting a few past lives and releasing the fear he experienced from getting lost, Sam's phobia of driving was gone.

A surprising result that occurred after releasing the shame in this life was the disappearance of his rheumatoid arthritis. As we worked together dealing with shame, his arthritis began to heal. His walking became better. By the end of the year, Sam's arthritis was completely gone. Shame had been the cause of it.

Lesson:

Self-love and self-worth

Awareness and Connection:

Most of Sam's embarrassing encounters with his dad, near or on the street, involved his father yelling at him in front of his friends, telling him to "be strong" and admonishing him as being stupid. This made him feel ashamed and frightened, and caused him to question all his abilities, including driving. The cellular memory of his friend dying beneath the trolley created the fear that his driving could cause serious harm to someone.

He experienced getting lost in multiple past lives, which he carried forward as the fear of getting lost in this one. After understanding and releasing the emotions in the stories that caused the phobia, Sam was no longer phobic. With a map in hand, he was not afraid to drive anywhere anymore.

Fears and Phobias

Claustrophobia

A forty-year-old man named George came into my office to work on a severe case of claustrophobia. He reported that he would go into a state of anxiety when he got beneath the covers in bed. He felt the same anxiety in elevators or places where he was confined. In obtaining his history, George revealed "the only trauma in his life" was a car accident during which he had been driving and which killed his best friend.

"I can't cover myself with my blanket."

Intention:

Let us go to the root of your claustrophobia.

George regressed to a medieval life, where he was a teenage girl in a field of flowers. She enjoyed being alone, isolating herself from others, without any thought of her vulnerability as a young woman.

While picking flowers, a huge man wearing a black cape and dark clothing kidnapped her and brought her to a large, stone house in a deserted countryside. Not even bothering to remove his black cape, he raped her. Afterward, he threw her in a deep hole in the ground, where she was bitten by rats and died within a week.

Lesson:

Strength

Awareness and Connection:

George realized that the blankets evoked the cellular memory of the black-caped man. The memory surfaced as a phobia. The hole that he had been thrown into triggered fears of enclosed spaces, causing the claustrophobia in this life.

I asked him if he recognized the energy of the caped man in this life. George was surprised when he realized it was his best friend, who had died in the car crash when George had been driving.

In the past life, George's friend had caused his death. In this life, George was responsible for his friend's death. I explained this as karmic balance. With this understanding, George was able to release the guilt he had been carrying since the accident.

George needed three more lifetime regressions to release his claustrophobia. After his first session, however, he was able to cover himself with blankets.

Fears and Phobias

Bridges

Susan came to me since she had had a bridge phobia for the last ten years. She claimed to know from where it originated. She had witnessed a truck crashing through a bridge rail and falling off the bridge into the water. It was a very traumatic event for her and caused her to feel faint and blurry-eyed every time she subsequently went over a bridge.

Susan had just accepted a job in Nyack, New York, requiring her to cross the Tappan Zee Bridge over the Hudson River every day. Jobs being scarce at the time, Susan had accepted the job offer but was in total anxiety about it.

This case was present-life problematic, so I decided to use a technique requiring a reframing of the incident.

"I saw the truck go off the bridge."

Intention:

I told a story that Susan gave me using her cues of when she would start to get symptomatic, where her anxiety would start, where it would peak, and when she would feel safe.

I narrated the story touch-anchoring (touching a spot on her hand) the peaked emotion. I retold it, then touching the safe emotion to anchor it. Next, I reversed the story, confusing either the anchors or order. During the next narration, I touched both anchors to further confuse the emotional state. Finally, I touched the positive anchor when she peaked with fear. This is an Ericksonian technique used for reframing.

I had Susan touch the safe anchor herself so she could feel the sense of calm. I told her if she needed an extra reinforcement, all she had to do was to touch the safe anchor and she would be fine.

Lesson:

Trust

(I asked her what she would learn from this experience, and she said that she needed to learn to trust herself that she could be strong and overcome the phobia.)

Awareness and Connection:

Susan was skeptical of the success she would have doing a fifteen-minute reframing technique. I told her she did not have to pay me until after she tried the bridge to see if it worked. Susan called me that day to ask what kind of magic this was since she had been perfectly fine going over the bridge—absolutely symptom-free. She thanked me profusely and sent out her check right away.

I saw Susan four years later and asked how she was doing with bridges. She said all was well, no more bridge phobia.

Fears and Phobias

Heights

Cathy, a grandmother about seventy-five years old, came to me about her height phobia. It had been getting worse over the last five years so that she could no longer even go down an escalator in a department store.

I asked her when it started, and she said since she was a little girl. She could never look down from a high place, never go up mountains or tall buildings. Her life had been somewhat sheltered from these places. She did love to shop, so this was putting a big hold on her shopping malls.

"I get so frightened when I am up high."

Intention:

I regressed Cathy back to the root of her height phobia.

Cathy described herself dressed in a beautiful *kimono* with her face painted white and her lips red. Her hair was in a lovely sculpture-like style, and she was taking very little steps as she walked.

She described the setting where a stream ran through the village with weeping willow trees and blossom trees adorning the stream. There was a small bridge connecting the town with the mountain on the other side. Many villagers would climb the mountain to pick tea and for exercise.

Cathy saw that she and her sister (who was her daughter in this life) were both *geisha* girls. They loved each other dearly and supported each other through their difficult careers.

Cathy hated what she was doing. She felt dirty and unworthy due to the pleasures she had to perform. Her sister in that life encouraged her, however, since they were fed well and dressed beautifully. She would tell Cathy that it was only a job, and this is what they were employed to do.

As time went on, Cathy could not take it anymore, so she climbed the mountain and leapt to her death. Her sister found her at the bottom of the mountain, dead.

Last Thoughts:

I cannot go on like this anymore. I hate my life. My work is degrading.

Lesson:

Strength

Awareness and Connection:

Cathy cried when she came around. She now understood from where her height phobia came. She died jumping off something high with great sadness and regret.

Cathy also realized why she always thought sex was a woman's job. She did not find pleasure in it and always felt dirty with her husband. She loved him but could never be truly intimate. She always wanted it to just be over.

In this life, Cathy's daughter worries about her mother and is always trying to protect her. She recalled her mother telling her when she got pregnant that it was a wife's job to satisfy her husband. Her daughter was sad her mother never found joy intimately.

Cathy made one more connection. The beautiful *kimonos* kept Cathy desiring beautiful clothes. She has always been drawn to Asian-style clothes.

Cathy said she could feel her height phobia lifting since she felt much lighter.

Fears and Phobias

<u>Disappearing</u>

Alice's mom called me to set up an appointment for her nineteen-year-old daughter who was dying of anorexia and who had dropped out of college because of an irrational fear of being focused upon. After trying all types of treatment, including hospitalization, my work was her last hope.

Alice began by explaining that she just wanted to disappear when anyone focused on her, whether a waiter asking for her order or a teacher asking her a question. Alice was disappearing by not eating.

"They are watching me!"

Intention:

Let us go to the root of Alice's fear of being focused on.

Under light trance, Alice regressed to a life in the 1930s in which she saw herself as a beautiful woman in a lovely gown walking down a large staircase to join a party. Everyone stared in awe of her beauty as she descended the stairs. She realized the party was to honor her for something we now call "best supporting actress."

I took Alice back in that life to a time in her childhood with her family. Her father, a big Hollywood producer, always asked Alice to perform for guests. Sometimes, he asked her to dance or sing for them. Alice hated being ordered by her father to perform for everyone.

When sent to a boarding school, Alice finally learned to like herself. After returning from school and no longer under pressure from her dad, she felt free to make her own decision to go to acting school. It was there that she fell in love and then married.

As Alice's ability as an actress began to grow, so did her career. This made her husband jealous since his career was not going anywhere. They began to quarrel, and he became abusive.

Still, Alice's career continued. Winning a prestigious award for her acting, she found herself at the party in her honor.

That evening, standing on the balcony, she and her husband began another fight. When he hit her, she fell over the balcony and died.

Last Thoughts:

None (Death came too quickly.)

Lesson:

Self-love

Awareness and Connection:

In order to heal from anorexia, Alice channeled that she should work with children, which would take the focus off her and put it on the children.

In Alice's memory of that earlier life, she recalled feeling wonderful walking down the stairs to greet her guests at the awards party thrown in her honor. However, her untimely death in a lifetime in which she had been the focus of others caused her to wish to disappear in this life before she would be killed.

Her desperate attempt to starve herself was her subconscious effort to protect herself from losing a life with which she connected. If she disappeared by losing weight, they would not be able to focus on her. This fear of being the center of attention caused her to starve herself, akin to killing herself. She loved being and feeling admired, but she feared dying a horrible death because of it. The irrational solution of trying to disappear became a horrific problem.

After a few months, Alice was showing results. Alice's mother was filled with gratitude, thanking me for saving her daughter's life. Alice was now eating healthy meals and doing well in school. She was moving toward a degree in early childhood education.

Fears and Phobias

<u>Dirt</u>

Heidi came to work on her fears or phobia about cleanliness. Ever since she could remember, she had always washed her hands before a meal without being told to do so. Even in the high-chair, she had wiped off crumbs using her sleeve. As a little girl, she pulled back the covers before she went to sleep, checking to see if there were hairs on her sheets.

Now that she had roommates, trying to keep her house clean with other people in her living space had heightened her fears and sent her over the edge.

"There's a hair in my bed."

Intention:

Let us go back to the root of your fear about uncleanliness.

Heidi regressed to a concentration camp, seeing herself in a bunk that was filled with filth, excrement, blood, urine, vomit, cut hair, and dirt. Heidi started to choke back her own vomit when she reported the stench in her bunk.

I regressed her to an earlier time in that life before the concentration camp. Sitting at the table around a meal in her lovely home, taking in the wonderful smells of her mother's cooking, she felt love and warmth. Her daily life was filled with the routine of school, and she had many friendships.

As we progressed, she described her parents' growing concern regarding politics around the country. They tried to protect her as things were changing, trying to keep her life the way it was.

When the Germans stomped into her home, pulling her mother, father, small brother, and herself from their house and forcing them into a truck, Heidi was shocked. She had no idea where they were going.

Along the way, she witnessed Jews shot in a line-up. She saw children pulled from their families. While Heidi and her mother were kept together in one bunker, her father and brother were taken somewhere else.

Everyone was given a job. Her job was to clean out the latrines. Once again, Heidi began gagging while she explained.

I progressed her five years. By then, she was no longer in the camp and now lived in a home with her new family. Her mother and brother had not been rescued but had died from starvation. She never knew if her father had survived or, if he had, where he was. At the time of her rescue, Heidi had been hiding in the feces-filled latrine.

Even though Heidi was freed from the camp, she was never freed from the horror. Seven years after her release, she committed suicide by hanging.

Last Thoughts:

I can't live anymore with these nightmares and depression.

Lesson:

Strength

Awareness and Connection:

Heidi understood her phobia about unclean places and the disgust she had experienced cleaning and later hiding in the latrine. The filth she had lived in was still vivid.

Her strange behavior, such as checking for hair in her sheets, became clear. She also understood why roommates, who brought her cellular memory of those with whom she had bunked in the past, intensified her fears and caused excessive anxiety about keeping her place clean.

We released the energy of fear around filth. Heidi reports that she is much better. She still likes to keep things clean, but her fear has disappeared.

Not only has her fear disappeared, but so have the nightmares she had as a child related to the concentration camp. While fears may be the result of more than one lifetime, this was the only life she had to revisit to clear this fear.

Fears and Phobias

<u>Stop Chewing!</u>

Valerie came to see me due to her fear or phobia about people chewing gum. She seemed to get furious when she would see or hear someone chewing gum, so much so that she punched a girl in class behind her who wouldn't stop when she asked her to. Valerie was suspended for a few weeks for the incident. She said it sounds silly, but it really gets to her.

"I just can't stand it!"

Intention:

Let's go to the root of your anger around gum chewing.

I regressed Valerie back to being a young teen in this life, seeing her mother yelling at her while snapping her gum, telling her that she was no good and always causing problems. While her mom was chewing her gum wildly, she hit Valerie upside the head for no reason. Valerie felt the punishment didn't fit the crime, for her mom did this because Valerie put the cookies away on the wrong shelf. Valerie didn't feel she was such a bad person, but her gum-chewing mom made her feel this way. We released the sadness and anger she felt from this wrongdoing and forgave her mom since she didn't know any better herself. She, too, had an abusive mom, who was her role model.

As we went forward to the next significant event that had to do with gum chewing, we saw Valerie's sister chewing as well. She said Valerie slammed the door when it was her; she was chewing away when Val got hit once again. Val asked her sister to stop chewing the gum, that it bothered her so, but her sister intentionally continued. Her sister was jealous of Val since she was the oldest and got most of the attention, even if it was negative.

I progressed Valerie once again to the next significant event, and she saw herself sitting in class, stressed out that her homework would be incomplete. The evening before, her father came home in a drunken stupor, so her sister and she had to hide until he fell asleep or be abused by him. Hiding in the closet, her younger sister was chewing gum again. It drove her mad!

By the time he fell asleep, it was very late, and Valerie's mom shuffled them off to bed.

The next day, Valerie's classmate behind her was chewing gum, and Valerie asked her to stop. She said no, so Valerie hauled off and punched her. She was suspended from school for a few weeks and would daily get her mother's wrath while the woman was chewing gum.

Valerie has learned to keep her anger inside and not lash out, but in doing so she has developed an ulcer. I helped Valerie release the anger, sadness, and fear associated with gum chewing and gave her subconscious suggestions that it could feel a calm and relaxed feeling instead of any other emotional feeling that might come up.

Last Thoughts:

None

Lesson:

Stand in your truth

Awareness and Connection:

Valerie was rather surprised to find that her gum phobia was coming from this life. It made a lot of sense to her since her abusive mother, father, and sister were always chewing gum. She associated the gum with abuse and making her feel ashamed of never doing anything right. We talked about her mother's lack of love and lack of a good role model, so she knew nothing different. We also discussed that her father was an alcoholic and never knew what he was doing but would hit first and ask later. Valerie got to see that she was never the "bad one" as she thought and that she no longer needed to associate gum chewing with her abusers and the emotions attached to that.

The next week Valerie came back to do some more work, and I noticed she was chewing gum. I asked her why, and she said she chews now to actually empower herself and to make good use of it. A great success story. We are now working on feelings of unworthiness.

CHAPTER FIVE

Children

Children come into life with many memories still available from their last lives and past lives, as well as the in-between lives. These memories sometimes come out in dreams, playtime, coloring, or when asked specific questions that trigger one of the cellular memories. It is all very natural to them.

Sometimes, it can be a repetitive nightmare or behavior that they are acting out. Many children have been classified with ADD/ADHD or behavioral problems and put on medication to deal with some of those issues. I believe we are given many things to help a suffering human deal with issues. However, we need to try every avenue before medicating our children and labeling them.

Past-life work is a quick way to see from where an issue comes since we deal with the subconscious memory under hypnosis. We ask to go to the root of the problem. It could also bring us back to our childhood in this life. It is the fastest way to uncover the problem.

Children

<u>War</u>

Ralph, a ten-year-old little boy, came to me for a few issues, but his mother was most concerned with his ADD, especially his lack of focus. He would daydream in class and get overwhelmed when he would be given many directions at the same time.

"I didn't see it coming."

Intention:

Let us go back to the root of your focus issues that contribute to your ADD. (The more specific we are with our intention, the more specific the memory.)

I regressed Ralph back to a lifetime in 1777, where he saw himself in the Battle of Saratoga. We went further back to see how his life manifested in case anything happened along the way that influenced his focus issues in this life.

Ralph saw his family that he identified as his family in this life, but his father was sterner in the past life. He went to school in a one-room schoolhouse and was not thrilled to be there. He liked riding horses and fishing instead.

As time went forward, Ralph saw himself enlisted in the army at sixteen years old. He was young and had a girlfriend, who was fearful of his enlistment. He assured her that he would be fine and come back to marry her.

Ralph went into battle, and, on a hill, he was killed by gunfire, "never seeing it coming." He said people were shouting orders all over and just shouting.

Confused by the different commands, he got hit by a barrage of bullets before he could react to the commands. He died in confusion and the shock of death. He said that it took a while to cross over since it happened so quickly. "I had to get my bearings."

Last Thoughts:

I didn't see it coming.

Lesson:

Trust

Awareness and Connection:

We released the fear and confusion around Ralph's death. I told him he no longer had to fear hearing directions, that they would not harm him in this life. I told him he could focus now on what directions were given to him and fulfill them with grace and ease.

Ralph's mother called to set up another appointment and told me he was much more relaxed in class, better able to hear and complete directions. His focus had improved, but we had learned that Ralph had four more lifetimes we needed to bring up in order to clear his ADD. We made another appointment.

Children

<u>Heart Transplant</u>

Jeffrey's mother brought him to see me, since he had been having so many problems with his twin sister. His mother explained that, even in utero, his sister had been kicking him as he was lying on part of her.

She explained that since the twin sister had come into this world, she had been angry and combative. She said that her daughter could not even cross a room without doing karate chops and kicks. She was always picking on her twin brother, physically and emotionally.

Jeffrey said he loves her but felt she hated him. Jeffrey was a very sweet ten-year-old who was also bullied in school. He also had ADD and felt it difficult to pay attention in school.

Jeffrey jumped with delight when asked if he would like me to bring him back to a previous life to determine why he and his sister decided to come into this lifetime as twins.

"She's always karate-chopping me!"

Intention:

Let us go back to the lifetime that brought you and your sister into this life as twins.

Jeffrey regressed back to a lifetime in the 1950s. He saw himself in a rather normal family but that he had to go to the doctor's office quite often. He was only ten but thought he might have had cancer.

As time went on, Jeffrey grew up and went to college— although still going to doctors. He realized it was not cancer but a heart problem.

When Jeffrey turned twenty years-old, he married. He had a few children by the time he was thirty years old.

At age thirty-five, Jeffrey had to have a heart transplant. His own heart could no longer serve him. He received the heart of a young girl. This girl was his twin sister in this life.

After she passed in the past life, she was mad to see that he got her heart and then died a few months later. He saw this when he passed.

Now with her heart in him—her heart also housed her soul—they came into this life with a split soul and were now twins. She carried her cellular memory of being angry at him for dying and wasting her heart. That was why she was so angry at him here.

We called his sister's soul in to ask forgiveness for leaving so quickly. I explained to Jeffrey and his mother that if they share this regression with his twin, she might be able to release her anger and become friends with him again. He was very excited to do so when he got home.

Last Thoughts:

None

Lesson:

Love

Awareness and Connection:

Jeffrey found it interesting that he had to go to the doctor's so much in the past life since he is so fearful of doctors and needles in this one.

He was also excited to tell his sister this story so she could be less angry. He now understood why they came in as twins and why she had been so angry at him. He would try harder to help her understand.

Jeffrey was moving to the South with his family. He was going to try to find a Past Life Regression therapist in his new town.

Children

School Phobic

Cynthia brought in Megan, a lovely twelve-year-old girl, who was sweet and a bit shy. Megan had always done well in school. She was an A-student who was also in many advanced placement classes. This year, Megan became school phobic. She was especially fearful of going to her first-period class, English, which she had always enjoyed. She started to feel that the teacher and other students in her class thought she was "stupid." She was also afraid that her mother would not be waiting for her after school and would leave her there.

None of these things ever happened to her, so Cynthia and Megan were baffled. When they came to me, Megan was able only to go to school and just sit in the guidance counselor's office. She could not go any further.

I asked Megan to tell me in her words what felt the most frightening to her. She said that not having her mother waiting for her after school was more frightening. So I decided that we would start with that fear. Her second fear was that her teacher and the students would think that she was stupid. The third fear was of first period and the bell going off.

"I used to like school."

Intention:

Let us go to the root of your fear around your mother not being there to pick you up after school.

I regressed Megan back to a life in the 1700s somewhere in the eastern part of the United States. She lived with her family: her mother, father, and sister.

Megan noticed that she was different. She felt like she did not belong or fit in. She saw herself as mentally handicapped. Her parents doted on her sister but seemed to ignore her.

At twelve years of age, they all went on a family picnic. After the picnic was over, they told her to stay and wait for them.

Megan waited for days, and they never came back for her. She did not know where she was and where to go, so she just started walking and walking for days.

Megan landed in a Native American village, where they took her in and treated her like one of their own. They learned about her deficits but gave her jobs watching the children or helping to prepare the food. They were very kind to her, more than her own family.

One day, Megan took the children down the road to the swimming hole. Upon returning to the village, Megan and the children hid since the village was being attacked. They waited until it was over and then ran as far away as possible. Megan tried to mother the children the best she could, but she knew that if she did not find them a new home, they would die.

The following day, they found their way to a town run by the white man. They made fun of Megan and the children. They forced them to work and do hard, laborious jobs for food and shelter. For years they stayed there until Megan got old and died from her hard life. The townspeople had grown to love and respect her, but they still considered her an Indian. She died with the townspeople all around her, feeling their love.

Last Thoughts:

I wonder what happened to my original family. At least I am loved now.

Lesson:

Trust

Awareness and Connection:

Megan found out that her family left her and never came back for her at the same age she was now in this life. Her age triggered these cellular memories.

Megan realized that her fear of her mother not being there for her after school was just a memory of a time long ago. Megan's mom was always there after school and promised to always be there for her in the future. The fear that her mom would not show up finally left.

Second Regression

Feeling Stupid and Fearful

Intention:

Let us go back to the lifetime that started this fear of feeling stupid and fearful.

I regressed Megan back to a lifetime in the 1800s, where she saw herself in a one-room schoolhouse. She described herself sitting in class with her teacher asking her a question and her not knowing the answer. The teacher pulled her up by her ear and dragged her out of the class, calling her stupid. The other children laughed at her and also called her stupid.

She admitted that she had a mental disability and really was stupid, but she still had her feelings hurt as she froze in fear. I helped Megan release the fear and sad feelings.

We progressed another five years, where we saw Megan still in class and feeling just as stupid and fearful. A few years later in her teens, Megan hanged herself since she could not bear the ridicule anymore.

Last Thoughts:

I cannot bear living anymore feeling so stupid and afraid.

Lesson:

Self-love

Awareness and Connection:

Megan realized that her fears were coming from that life and affecting her life here all of a sudden. I explained that she was now close to the same age as when she was traumatized at school and had committed suicide in that previous life. Her cellular memories were triggered by her age. Megan was so relieved to hear this that, making the connection, she no longer felt stupid. That symptom disappeared.

One by one, the fears started to slip away.

Third Regression

Fire!

Intention:

Let us go back to the root of your fear around first period and bells or alarms going off.

I regressed Megan back to a lifetime in the 1920s. She was having a special day at school, where she was presenting a book report to the class and parents. Megan was proud and excited to have her mother and father at her school and proud to share her report.

Just as Megan started to give her report, the fire alarm went off. The school was on fire. Megan and the children were told to leave immediately, and the parents were to follow. After the children left, the flames engulfed the school, and the parents were trapped inside. Megan's parents died in the fire.

Megan felt so sad and responsible. She grew up with her cousins but remained quiet and depressed. She died of an illness as a young woman.

Last Thoughts:

I do not want to live anymore.

Lesson:

Self-love

Awareness and Connection:

Megan could not believe how the parents came in her first-period English class for her report and then died in a fire. It was so specific. Once again, Megan was twelve years old when this event took place in her past life. Once again, her cellular memory was picking up so many memories of different lifetimes all in her twelfth year and all having to do with school and her mental abilities.

Megan did not want to do the last two regressions since the first felt so hard for her. However, she mustered up the courage. After the healing, she was grateful for the intervention.

Megan went back to school shortly after our work. She went back to being a good student once again but now with no fear.

It is amazing that we may have more than one lifetime affecting the same issue that we develop out of the blue. We sometimes need to peel away one lifetime after the next until the issue is cleared.

The language of the child was critical to the intention we went seeking, since each one was very specific to the issue. The timing of the events was also critical, since they all happened at her present age.

Children

Nightmares

A lovely Mexican woman named Maria called me to see if I could help her son, Thomas, who was six years old and having nightmares about wars. She also told me that he was having trouble in school, pushing children in line behind him or getting out of circle-time in the classroom by hiding on either side of the room. The teachers had classified him as having ADD/ADHD. She was more concerned about his nightmares, since they always disrupted his sleep.

"They shot me in the back!"

Intention:

Due to the age of the child and since most young children go into trance easily, especially when drawing, I asked Thomas if he could draw me a picture of the nightmares. Thomas was very eager to draw the picture since he loved to draw in general.

He drew a picture of a trench on one side of the paper with two soldiers in that trench firing on two soldiers in another trench on the other side of the paper. There was a soldier dead in the middle with blood coming out. He also drew a helicopter in the sky with two missiles on it.

When I asked Thomas who were the men in the first trench, he said, "They are the Chinese!" When asked who the soldiers in the other trench were, he said, "They are the Russians!" When I asked which side he was on, he said, "I am the Chinese." I asked him if he died in that war, and he said no.

I asked Thomas where he went after the war, and he turned over the page of drawing paper and drew a picture of a small pagoda, two stick figures, a little arched bridge over a stream, and a single stick figure further down the property. When asked where this was, he said, "This is my house. These are my parents, and this is me."

When asked if he died there, he said no. I asked him where he died, and he turned over the next page of the drawing pad and drew rows of tombstones with the rain coming down.

As he pointed to one of the tombstones and said, "There I am."

I asked him, "How did you die?" He said, "They shot me in the back!"

I asked who shot him. He did not know.

Last Thoughts:

I had none since it all happened so fast.

Lesson:

Not sure

Awareness and Connection:

Thomas remembered that the war in his dreams looked very similar to the drawings. Thomas's mom called to tell me that his teacher called home a couple of weeks later to tell her that Thomas was no longer pushing on line and that he now sat still in the circle activities. They were going to withdraw their classification of him having ADD/ADHD. No medication was necessary.

Thomas had had no history education yet in school, especially concerning the Chinese or Russians. After all, he was a little Mexican boy who barely knew the history of the United States. Yes, there had been a Chinese-Russian conflict involving helicopters.

Thomas's nightmares had also stopped immediately as well. One should try all avenues before treating children with medications.

Children

Auschwitz

Liza, an eight-year-old little girl, came to see me with her mom about her sleeping issues. Apparently, since the time Liza was able to talk, she would cry every night at bedtime, always repeating, "Don't leave me; something is going to happen to you."

Every night, Liza's mom had to sit in the bedroom with Liza until she would fall asleep. If Liza awoke in the night, she would come into her mother's room, either climbing into bed with her or sliding into a sleeping bag on the floor.

As Liza got older, the sleeping issues rippled out into other areas of their life. When Liza's parents wanted to go out to dinner or a movie alone, Liza would cry out the same thing, "Don't go! Something is going to happen to you." It was most pronounced at bedtime. It also happened only in association with her mother and not with her father.

"Don't leave me!"

Intention:

Let us go back to the root of what is making you so fearful that something is going to happen to your mom.

Liza regressed back to being on a train on the way to Auschwitz. She described the train car being stuffed with people. She was fifteen years old there. When they reached the camp, they took Liza and her mother to a building where both had their hair shaved off.

She said her mother was so terrified that she wanted "to do suicide." Liza said she had to stay up at night to make sure her mother would not attempt to do so. By the third night, Liza could not stay up any longer and fell asleep. Her mother then ran out and tried climbing over the fence, where she was shot and killed.

There it was: if I go to sleep, my mother will die. This is what Liza carried in her cellular memory right into this life.

Liza actually survived the camp, married, and had a daughter. When her daughter turned four years old, they went rowing in a boat on a lake. Liza's daughter went overboard. Liza jumped in to try to save her, but they both drowned.

Last Thoughts:

None (Could not remember.)

Lesson:

Strength

Awareness and Connection:

I was a bit fearful how a child of eight years old would handle such a traumatic lifetime. How could she process this? Liza came out of the regression and jumped up, saying, "Now I understand why I was always so worried about my mom." She proceeded to skip out of my office. Liza's mom and I were both so relieved.

Liza's mom called me two weeks later to report that Liza no longer came into her room at night and stopped saying, "Don't leave me. Something is going to happen to you." She said the change happened almost instantaneously. That night, she stayed in her own room and continued to do so from then on.

A month later, Liza's mom called to tell me that Liza had started to stall at night, asking for water or saying that she had to go to the bathroom. She told me that they were in the midst of changing Liza's bedroom from a bunk bed to a double bed. She reported that after the change took place, the stalling stopped. Liza had been holding some cellular memory around the bunk bed, since it reminded her of the beds in Auschwitz. After the bunk bed was gone, the memory also left, as well as the stalling. Liza now goes to sleep with peace and joy.

Children

<u>The Showers</u>

Chris came to my office with his mother, since Chris was only three years old. His mother told me that any time her son had to go to the bathroom and smelled any excrement, he would throw up.

It had become a huge problem once Chris started nursery school. At bathroom time, some of the children would have bowel movements, and Chris would have a violent reaction and throw up. The teacher was horrified and asked that he not attend school until he could stop this reaction. Chris's mother pleaded with me to help.

"I can't stand the smell."

Intention:

Chris, can you draw me a picture of when you go to the bathroom and when the smells make you sick?

Chris was only three years old, so traditional ways of accessing memories would not work. Children go into trance while drawing.

Chris could only scribble, so I asked a series of questions while he scribbled.

Chris's mother remembered that she had done a regression with me in which she was in the Holocaust. Chris had been her son in that life, too, and had been led naked to the "showers" with the others to be killed. He was small enough to have his face almost shoved against the butt of the man in front of him.

I used this information to prod Chris whether he hated the smell due to walking as a little boy so close to a man who was naked and may have smelled badly. I told him he did not have to throw up anymore but could bring a small bottle of air freshener or perfume into the bathroom and smell that instead. Chris just kept smiling and scribbling.

I was not sure if Chris was too young to change his behavior but asked his mother to keep me informed.

Awareness and Connection:

Chris's mother called me the following week to inform me that he had not thrown up since our session. He now carries the small perfume bottle to school and at home and seems just fine.

She was so happy and could not believe that the session worked on such a young child. I, too, was surprised since I was not sure I was getting in there. Bringing the memory to his consciousness while he was in trance and drawing was enough to clear cellular blockages. The use of a perfume bottle for smell and for an anchor to his new behavior was enough to create a change.

CHAPTER SIX

Weight Issues

Weight is one of the most complex and prevalent issues that regressionists see in clients who come through their offices. There are many reasons we eat, and many others why we do not. We need to "fill a void," reward good or bad behavior, seek revenge, cope with anxiety or boredom, deal with self-anger, etc.

In the following case histories, readers may find the root of their own issues so that they, too, can move past resistance to good health. These histories will help the reader understand the complexity and contributing factors of weight issues. If you have been unsuccessful in past weight-loss attempts, releasing the emotions that cause the issue may be the answer.

Weight Issues

Always Traveling

Janet came to my office for help with her weight issue. Apparently, her husband had to travel all the time for business. Janet is a mother of three young children. She had no outside help, so she had to take care of the home and children all by herself. Janet was constantly finishing her children's food, rationalizing it so as to avoid waste. She was also constantly eating snacks as a source of energy to keep her going during the day. She realized that she was taking in more calories than she was burning up, but she felt that with all she had to do, she should be thin. As a result, she was frustrated and felt hopeless.

"Let's not waste the food!"

Intention:

Let us go back to the lifetime affecting your eating issues.

Janet regressed back to a lifetime in England. She saw herself as a woman of twenty-five years old, making a dinner of potatoes for her four children. Janet said her husband had died of a disease last year, and she had to take care of her children alone. Janet would take in laundry to wash and iron for the little bit of food or money she could get.

When Janet was a small child of ten, she saw herself helping her mother clean for a wealthy family. Janet's father had died when she was two years old from a farming accident, so the family let them live in the same house in exchange for cleaning the house. Janet worked all day with her mother and was exhausted at the end of the day from the hard work. This went on for years until Janet was eighteen.

At that time, Janet met a farmer who fell in love with her and married her. Janet was finally happy that she would have someone to rescue her from the hardship she endured with her mother.

At age twenty, Janet was finally getting used to farm life with two children to care for in addition. She did the farm chores and carried her children around, taking care of them as well.

At age twenty-four, Janet had two more children, when her husband also had an accident and died. She could not take care of the farm and the children, so she moved to the city, where she lived in an apartment, washing and ironing clothes for other people. It paid for her rent and barely enough for food to feed her family. She ate little so they could eat. She worked always feeling weak and frail.

By age thirty, Janet was dying of malnutrition and dehydration. Her fears were about her children; who would take care of them and feed them? She was so tired; all she wanted to do was leave so she would not have to worry anymore.

Janet died with her children all around her.

Last Thoughts:

Who will care for my children?

Lesson:

Self-love

Awareness and Connection:

Janet felt that she came into this life with almost the same drama — only instead of her husband dying, leaving her to fend for herself, kids, and the home, he travels now. She still has to do the same.

She also connected that food has been so important to her here since she was always hungry, never had enough, and was always giving the food to her children first. Now, she finishes her children's food so as not to waste it, her cellular memory reminding her she may not get any in the future.

The snacks in this life give Janet the energy to get through the day, which she never had in the last life. The snacks also act as a reward for the hard work she is doing in this life.

In addition, she had an insight that the snacks were also filling the void of her husband's absence. She asked her husband for someone to come in and help her a few afternoons with the children so she could have a little time for herself to just rest or exercise. He agreed that they could afford it, so Janet finally started having hope she could have more will power to lose her weight.

I gave Janet a suggestion while under that she no longer needed to eat in fear of not having enough but could eat to enjoy, thus limiting the amounts to healthy and reasonable portions. Also, she did not need to fear starving in this life, for it was only cellular memory that caused her to feel that.

Weight Issues

Bulimia

Antonia came to see me with low self-esteem issues and a need to always purge after eating. She told me she would be hungry and eat too much or something really good and then feels terribly guilty about it and need to throw it up. When we discussed it further, it seemed that Antonia had a beautiful sister who was very thin, smart, and adored by their mother. No matter what Antonia would do to win her mother's admiration, the mother would always hold her sister up on a pedestal.

In trying to compete for her mother's love, Antonia felt she had to be thin and beautiful, too. When she ate, she felt guilty. Since she needed to lose weight, she would purge and get rid of what was coming between her relationship with her mother.

"I should not have eaten it. I have to get rid of it!"

Intention:

Let us go to the root of your bulimia.

Antonia regressed back to a life in Mexico in the 1700s. She saw herself as a poor, young girl in rags, begging for money or food. She saw that she had seven siblings younger than she. It was her earnings that would mean food or hungry bellies.

Her mother would constantly tell her that her efforts were not good enough and that she had better do well that day or she would get a smaller portion.

If Antonia could not get enough for the day, her portion was given to the rest of the family so that they could eat, telling her it was her fault there was not enough.

When Antonia turned twenty, she prostituted herself in the local bar to get enough money to feed her family. She so wanted to have her mother's love and approval from the earnings of her work. For poor Antonia, it was always about what everyone else needed or wanted but never for herself. If she would get something pretty or tasty, she would give it to her siblings or mother right away. Her own desires were met with guilt and the feeling that she did not deserve anything since she was supposed to take care of her family.

At age thirty-five, Antonia died from venereal disease, hungry and unappreciated by her family, who felt she had let them down.

Last Thoughts:

Now my family will starve. I wish they could have seen how hard I tried.

Lesson:

Self-love

Awareness and Connection:

Antonia was so sad that she always tried so hard yet was so unappreciated. She identified the mother as the same in this life. She realized that she is still trying to please her and working so hard at it. The guilt of not having enough has made her purge anything good or nurturing for herself.

She saw that her family in the past life was so spoiled and depended solely on her for their survival. They should have made their own way. The mother never saw beyond what she wanted and still does not today. Antonia realized that she does not have to give up one more thing for this family, for they do not reciprocate or appreciate her here in this life as well.

Antonia pledged that she would try to eat healthier and do more nurturing things for herself. She realized that she is thin and beautiful enough, and she is happy with that.

Antonia had four more lifetimes to release from in order to clear her issue of bulimia.

Weight Issues

Depression

Sophie came to me in what she described as a chronic depression. She had been depressed since she was a small child. She always had issues with her mother. She was somewhat overweight but did not seem too affected by it. Sophie had a great sense of humor but inside she carried great sadness.

"I killed my mother with an axe."

Intention:

Let us go back to the root of your depression.

Sophie regressed back to a lifetime in the 1800s. She described a small village in the Midwest, where she lived in a small house surrounded by a picket fence. The house was within walking distance to the town, which she loved going to as a small child.

Sophie identified her mother as her mother in this life. She loved to bake and loved Sophie to taste and enjoy everything she made. Sophie's father was a rather quiet man who always sat in the living room or parlor, reading the paper. The mother ruled the roost.

As Sophie grew up, her mother demanded that her daughter continue to eat all that she cooked. Sophie started to get heavier and heavier, and the children at school made fun of her weight. Sophie was so embarrassed and asked her mother for help so she could lose weight, but her mother's obsession with cooking and feeding her blocked any help and just continued to feed the problem.

When Sophie reached eighteen years of age—the age to find a suitor—she had gotten so large that no men were interested.

Her mother would yell at her that she was so heavy and that no man wanted her, yet she continued to cook and feed her.

Sophie's father died that year, leaving Sophie with her obsessed, shrewish mother, who became even more abusive as time went on. She continued to blame Sophie for eating too much and not being attractive enough to catch a man.

At twenty-five years old, Sophie could no longer take the abuse and snapped. She picked up an axe and cut her mother's head off so she would stop yelling at her.

Sophie had no remorse or understanding of what she had done. She buried her mother and told the town that her mother left to visit relatives.

Sophie never married, but she secretly did the bookkeeping for the general store. She survived on that income and continued to cook for herself, not caring what she looked like.

Sophie died of natural causes at age seventy-five.

Last Thoughts:

Thank God my mother is gone.

Lesson:

Speak your voice

Awareness and Connection:

Sophie was shocked that she had cut her mother's head off without remorse. She understood why she and her mother were always at odds with each other in this life. She saw that due to feeling so trapped between her mother's obsessive behavior with food, and her inability to make real friends, she snapped.

Never having resolved her depression from that life, Sophie carried it here again with the same nemesis: her mother. Eating her mother's food and thus pleasing her mother resulted in her getting the only approval in her life.

We discussed how releasing these feelings of entrapment, depression, and punishment would help heal her depression as well as her issue of eating for approval.

Sophie was rather unnerved by seeing herself cut her mother's head off. I explained that we have all been the abuser and have all been the abused. When we snap from constant abuse, we do things that are not always in our rational minds. We learn from these tragic events so that they will not happen again in our next incarnations.

Sophie also realized how important it is to speak up for oneself and not allow a person to abuse us. Sophie has a mastery of language here and is a great writer. She feels she has come into this life to learn how to express herself in a more appropriate way.

Weight Issues

<u>An Old Man</u>

Patty came to see me, disillusioned that no matter what she did, she just could not lose weight. She explained that she was pretty thin or average until she started approaching her fifties. At that time, she had become depressed when she found out that her mother had died alone. She felt guilty that she had not been there to comfort her at her death.

When her depression started, her overeating began. She realized she had been trying to fill the void from the loss of her mother. She mostly ate things like popcorn, pretzels, chips, and cookies. She felt she could keep popping these foods in until she felt full. Even with this acknowledgment, she just could not stop filling herself with these foods.

"I never harvested enough for my old age."

Intention:

Let us go back to the root of your eating issues.

Patty saw herself as an old Hawaiian man standing by the water, watching a beautiful sunset. When asked how she felt standing there, she said, "Sad and frightened."

Patty saw herself growing up in a loving family who were good hunters and fishermen. They always had food on the table, love, and joy. She also saw that they were part of a very loving community.

The community had its set of rules, which included that each family had to provide food and shelter for themselves. Patty's family had no problem, since she came from a large family with four siblings. Patty was the youngest and somewhat weaker than her siblings, so they always made sure she had enough to eat.

Growing up, Patty saw that, due to her kind siblings, she became very lazy. As her siblings moved and spread out in the village, they encouraged Patty to try harder in her fishing and hunting.

One of the siblings took in their parents to care for, leaving Patty to fend for herself. Patty barely fed herself since she did not want to work so hard. She became very thin but lived until seventy years old. That is when Patty saw herself at the water's edge, thinking about how she should have worked harder and harvested more for her old age.

A few years later, Patty died of starvation after being too lazy and too proud to ask for help. She saw her family carry her on a burning pyre surrounded by flowers, which was set in the water in order to go to a natural grave. Patty got to see her family mourn and the great sadness they had for her loss.

Last Thoughts:

Due to my laziness and lack of harvesting, I starved to death.

Lesson There:

Self-reliance and hard work

Lesson Here:

Worthiness

Awareness and Connection:

Patty cried watching her family mourn her death. It reminded her of her own feelings when her mother died. This association triggered her cellular memory to eat since she had died of starvation in that life.

We discussed how Patty need not fill her void with food but can instead know she will always be prepared here so she will not starve to death in this life.

We also discussed how she could accomplish more constructive ways to remember her mom. She decided to put together an album of all the loose pictures of their life together that she found in a box. We discussed how Patty was not at fault for not being present with her mother when she passed. Sometimes our family member may decide to wait until we leave to pass, since they feel it may be too hard on their loved ones or on their own letting go.

Patty was finally able to put closure to her mother's death and find a healthy way to process and to eat.

Weight Issues

<u>Protection</u>

Hollie came to see me in order to lose weight. At twenty-five years old, she was very quiet and reluctant to answer questions.

When I took a history intake, I found that Hollie had been sexually abused by her uncle. She felt very ashamed even though it happened from when she was six years old until her teenage years.

Somehow, Hollie still blamed herself for the awful things her uncle did to her. When asked, Hollie reported that she started gaining weight when she was nine years old and has been heavy since.

I explained to Hollie that many times when one has been abused, one gains the weight for protection. She agreed but knew she would feel better at this time of her life if she lost the weight so she could feel attractive. All of her efforts had failed so far.

"He hurt me!"

Intention:

Let us go back to the root of your weight issues.

Hollie went back to a lifetime as a harem girl. She was one of twenty-six wives. She was happy she did not have to please her master daily.

When we went back to when Hollie was ten years old, she had already been sold to a family of nobility. From ten to thirteen, she was being groomed for her position as another wife. Hollie did not like her master, for he was big, hairy, and smelly. He was also rough with her and frightened her. She identified the master in her past life as the same man who abused her in this one.

At age twenty, Hollie became the second wife of favor. Her master would call on her to perform sexual acts for him that were painful to her. She would cry and try to run away, but he found and beat her before having his way with her.

At twenty-five years old, Hollie could take no more, so she hanged herself in the gardens.

Last Thoughts:

I want to die; I can take no more.

Lesson:

Trust

Awareness and Connection:

Hollie realized that she could not trust her uncle in this life. She explained that her family in this life was Italian and felt family was stronger and more important than anything else. Hollie felt that her family could be trusted and would not let her down — until her uncle started to abuse her.

Her parents did not believe Hollie and told her to stop making up these lies. In this life, those who Hollie trusted betrayed her and abandoned her during her time of need. Where were those strong family ties of which she had heard? Was she so worthless that her parents would believe her abuser over her?

In the past life, Hollie found no way to deal with her constant abuse. The only way she felt she could control it in this life was to gain weight so her uncle would not find her appealing. It worked for Hollie, and her uncle has since passed away.

Hollie has used the weight as protection in this life and is afraid to let it go for fear the abuse may come back again.

Hollie and I worked on releasing all the trauma around the past-life events that contributed to her Karma here. We also worked on the feelings of unworthiness in this life and have been going back to all of the lifetimes connected to abuse and unworthiness. In understanding where this Karma has come from, Hollie felt hopeful that she could move on free of that trauma and Karma, and discern whom she can trust. She said she would never let anyone hurt her again.

Weight Issues

Last Meal

Larry came to see me, since his doctor told him that he must lose weight or he would die of a heart attack. Larry was well over three hundred pounds and had difficulty breathing. He told me that he loved food but felt he had to hide his food and then eat it when no one is around due to their judging him. He would take loaves of bread and hide them under his bed and then eat them before sleeping.

While he would feel guilty afterward, he felt he had better eat it just in case he could not tomorrow. He had no idea from where this feeling came, but he had had it since he was a small boy.

"Hide the bread."

Intention:

Let us go back to the root of your weight issue.

I regressed Larry back to a lifetime in Austria. He saw himself as a twelve-year-old boy in shorts with suspenders made of suede. He was happy up in the mountains, hiking with some friends.

Larry lived in the mountains in a small chalet-style home. His grandmother, his mother, and their dog lived there with him. His father was killed in an avalanche when Larry was four. They lived a simple life, growing their own food, hiking a lot, and having Friday night dinners together for Shabbat. They were grateful for all that they had.

When Larry turned fifteen years old, they were on their way to a concentration camp, huddled together in a truck. He was very scared but felt he needed to be the one to protect his mother and grandmother. When they got to the camp, Larry was separated from them and felt a tremendous amount of guilt.

Larry was very strong and was used by the Germans to haul heavy items in the camp. He barely ate since food was scarce, and the smells of filth, urine, feces, blood, and death were all around.

He brought wood for the fireplace of the captain's home, and he was rewarded with pieces of bread. He hid the bread in his pockets until back in the barracks. Just before bed, he nibbled on the bread while holding his breath due to the rancid smells. No one saw him eat it; otherwise, they would try to take it away for themselves. Everyone was so hungry. He could not share it, for it would cause chaos.

Larry felt guilt that his mother and grandmother probably had nothing to eat. He wished he could share the little he had with them. He was not even sure they were still alive.

One day, Larry was hauling some metal on a wagon when he spotted his mother. She was digging in the field when he saw her. He went by and whispered in her ear that he had some bread and would bring it to her that night. She told him where she was staying, and they agreed on a time and place.

That night, Larry sneaked off to meet his mother and was caught on the way. The soldier found the hidden bread in his coat and demanded that he be shot. While holding the bread, and much to his surprise, Larry was shot and killed.

Last Thoughts:

I should have hidden the bread better. Now we will starve.

Lesson:

Forgiveness

Awareness and Connection:

Larry realized why he always had to hide his food, especially the loaves of bread under his bed. Also, he now understood why he had to secretly eat them at night. Larry now understood why food was so important to him in this life, since he never knew when he would have another meal.

I pointed out that Larry held his breath in that life when eating due to the awful smells. In this life, being so heavy has made it difficult to breathe, as well. His cellular memory told him if he ate, he should not breathe.

We also discussed that he could not eat the bread in front of anyone or they would want it and take it away from him. They would judge him since no one else got food but him. Again, that was from where his fear of judgment concerning food came.

Larry felt guilt that his mother and grandmother would starve, so he carried that guilt into this life whenever he would eat. He admitted that his greatest fear was being caught with the loaves of bread under his bed.

Once Larry knew from where his obsessive fears about food came, he breathed a huge sigh of relief. He realized he no longer needed to hide his food since no one would take it away. He also did not need to eat like he better get it all in today since there may not be food tomorrow.

Larry finally developed a way of eating—not a "diet," which represents deprivation but a way to eat moderately and only at a table. He is down twenty pounds and feeling blessed to be alive, healthy, and free.

Weight Issues

Revenge

Sharon came to see me to determine if I could help her with her issues around losing weight. She had been on every diet "known to mankind."

She would lose some weight but always gain it back. Her husband kept telling her that she needed to lose weight to make her more appealing to him sexually. When she got angry at him for hurting her, she would tend to eat more. She said she would hear herself say, "I'll show him," and eat whatever she wanted. Later in life, her husband would use health as the reason she needed to lose weight, but Sharon would just eat more. She felt it was her husband who was the main reason for her weight problems.

"I'll show him."

Intention:

Let us go back to the root of your weight issues.

I regressed Sharon back to a lifetime in France in the 1700s. She saw herself as a tall, painfully thin woman with "very tall hair." She said that she was actually quite unattractive. This surprised Sharon since she was overweight in this life but had a very pretty face.

Sharon's father in the past life was her husband in this one. Her father would eat like a glutton, shoveling the food into his mouth. Disgusted, Sharon would barely eat in that life. When the time came for her to marry in that previous life, her father hounded her to eat more, since "no man wants to marry a skinny woman."

Sharon was amused that her father was frustrated at her thinness. He gave many parties for her in order to create opportunities to meet men. Sharon would go reluctantly because she realized the men were there to please her father and seek to marry her, the heir to the family fortune. They all lied to her, telling her that she was so beautiful and charming.

Sharon finally found a man whom she thought was honest, but when she probed further, she found that he, too, was only using her.

As her father continued to tell her to gain more weight in order to attract a suitor, she ate less and less with intention for revenge: "I'll show him!"

This went on for a couple of years, and, at age eighteen, Sharon died of what we would call today anorexia.

Last Thoughts:

I'll show him.

Lesson:

Self-love and forgiveness

Awareness and Connection:

Sharon realized that she has the same reaction here with her husband. Whenever he mentioned her weight, regardless if it related to her looks or her health, she felt the same resentment and desire for revenge.

This only hurt her in the long run, as in the past life, for she was killing herself once again. This time, she could die of a heart attack, diabetes, or even organ failure instead of anorexia. She realized that she needed to listen to and love herself, not listen to her husband. This time, Sharon would speak her voice to her husband, letting him know that his remarks were only adding fuel to the fire and not helping her in a constructive, loving way.

Sharon's husband began to understand the syndrome he created for her and decided to help by not mentioning her dieting or losing weight and by showing her he loved her unconditionally. He was willing to help her in any way she felt appropriate.

Sharon was grateful for his understanding and for her own. She wanted to learn her lesson well and stop contributing to her potential death. She went on a reasonable diet and exercise program, losing the weight slowly and lovingly. She also began to feel a new sense of self-worth and power behind speaking her voice.

Weight Issues

<u>Don't look!</u>

Joe came to see me, looking rather shy and like the cat that just swallowed the canary. He kept looking around like I might have someone hiding under my desk or behind the couch. He told me that he was a bit paranoid and that his problem was that he could never eat in front of anyone since he felt like they were always judging him. He said he thought they would think he should diet or not eat what he likes since it was probably not healthy for him. I asked if anyone in this life ever judged him that way, and he said no; he wasn't sure why he felt that way. He told me he stores food in his bedroom and hides some under his bed or in his drawers. He likes to eat at night when no one is around.

"I don't want them to judge me."

Intention:

Let's go back to the root of what is making you feel like everyone's judging you while you eat.

Joe regressed back to when he was a small child, three years old, in this lifetime. He was staying with his grandparents when his parents went on a vacation for the week. He remembers his grandfather yelling at his grandmother, and she was crying. I asked why he was yelling at her, and he said that she was fat and all she wanted to do was to fatten him up, as well as the rest of the family. He said she would die of a heart attack if she kept it up and would kill the rest of them. As I moved to the next significant event, he saw himself as a chubby young boy in first grade with the kids making fun of him, calling him fat and laughing at him. He started to cry in my chair, and I helped him release more of his sadness and shame. The next significant event was at a "fat camp" when he was twelve years old. He saw that they gave the kids small portions and made him do excessive amounts of exercise. He also had one counselor who would always tell him he would be watching him, and, if he cheated, they would take away the fruit dessert. Joe would always look over his shoulder to see if that counselor was around. Joe did lose the amount of weight he wanted, very careful to show everyone he had discipline.

Joe is in his thirties now and still a good weight. He is just fearful that he will be watched and judged and have someone control his food intake. During camp, Joe was always hungry. He could never eat what or when he wanted. When he came home from camp, he swore no one would ever control or judge his weight or food. He stopped eating in front of people so they would think he had great discipline and not bother him about his food. At night, he would eat what he wanted and with no one bothering him. Lucky for him, his metabolism is more efficient now, so he does not gain any weight.

Last Thoughts:

None

Lesson:

Standing in his truth

Awareness and Connection:

Joe realized how his whole life and the people in it were always negatively judged by their size. Since he was able to keep his body in shape over the last decade, he forgot why he was still hiding his food. Joe laughed and said no one has the right to judge anyone and that now he was old enough to tell them so. He didn't want to tell me the truth about his childhood, for he felt I would judge him as well. He thought if we found it under hypnosis, that would be fine. He realized that he needed help but was too ashamed to let on that he knew where it was coming from.

We released the sadness, shame, and anger he had held on to and filled that space with light and love. Joe was now in control.

CHAPTER SEVEN

Victimization

At some point of time in life, we all experience victimization. It can be severe, as with rape or incest, or mild, such as being the recipient of a verbally abusive boss. We have chosen this role in order to learn an important lesson.

Chapter Seven will share eight more sessions that will provide enlightenment on each person's story, which came from their difficult paths.

Victimization

Abuse

Simone came to me after many years of psychotherapy with the same burning questions that most people who are abused ask: Why me? Why did I have to go through this?

"Why did this have to happen to me?"

Intention:

Let us go back to the life that brought you into this lifetime causing you to be sexually abused by your father.

I regressed Simone to a lifetime on a plantation. She was a young male slave named Abraham. At ten, Abe went hunting with a group of men, helping to carry the killings.

While the men were busy readying the dogs for the hunt, Abe saw an opportunity to escape. As he started running down the path, one of the men saw him and yelled, "Boy loose!" The men sent the dogs to chase Abe. When he was caught, he was brought back to the plantation, where he was whipped, beaten, sexually sodomized, and thrown into a hole to die.

After everyone left, an old black woman took Abraham to her cabin, where she fed him and tended to his wounds. Abe was grateful to this woman but died feeling angry and defeated.

Last Thoughts:

I will never let him beat me again.

Lesson:

Strength and speaking his truth

Awareness and Connection:

Simone finally understood why she chose abuse again. As Abraham, she could not speak up for herself, and all she could have done was run away.

In this life, Simone can finally stand up for her rights and dignity and express herself. A musician, Simone coordinates benefits for abused women and children, using her talent as a singer to raise funds. She has created a CD of all her past lives, where she was learning to stand up to her abuser and speak her voice. Her question of "Why me?" had been answered.

Victimization

Always Ill

Rachel came to see me feeling frustrated and sad that she always seemed ill in this life without any breaks. She wanted to understand why.

Rachel complained about always having some type of illness or malady, never getting a break. She has had most of her female organs removed, stomach pains and diarrhea, congestive heart failure, spinal disk problems, psoriasis, breast cancer metastasized, diabetes, weight issues, and many more aliments. She has had every surgery, taken every pill, seen doctors on a daily basis, and yet she never seems to get better, only worse. In addition, Rachel has instigated four malpractice claims, for doctors always seem to make mistakes with respect to her. She asked why bad things always had to happen to her.

"I will never be well. I just can't get a break."

Intention:

Let us go back to the root of why you are constantly ill in this life.

I regressed Rachel back to a lifetime in the 1920s, where she was an only child growing up with alcoholic parents. They fought all the time, throwing plates, yelling obscenities, and slamming doors. Rachel was frightened as a child. There were times when her father locked her in a closet just so as not to have to deal with her.

At fifteen years old, Rachel left home and became a maid, cleaning houses for a living.

At sixteen years old, she married a man who was also an alcoholic. He, too, was abusive.

At seventeen, Rachel became pregnant, so she had to stop cleaning houses. Instead, she took in laundry to wash in order to help support them.

When her son was born, Rachel's husband left, never to return. She kept saying, "He was a no-good drunken bum" to her son when he was a baby and as he continued growing up. Rachel warned her son he would be just like his dad if he did not listen.

As soon as her son could crawl, Rachel would hit him for every little thing, day after day. When Rachel's son went to school, he was beat up by the boys for living on the wrong side of the tracks. When he came home, Rachel beat him for fighting with the boys.

She hated her son since he always reminded her of her husband. Rachel's rage grew stronger as her son grew older.

When her son turned fifteen, Rachel became ill. All of her rage turned inward against her, for she developed stomach cancer that finally destroyed her.

Even after all of her abuse, her son stayed by her bed, taking care of Rachel until she finally died.

Last Thoughts:

I just want to go. Death has to be better than life.

Lesson:

Forgiveness

Awareness and Connection:

In her previous life, Rachel was abused as a child and continued the cycle on her own child. She could have chosen to be a better mother than her own had been. Since her husband also abused her, Rachel knew abuse and taking anger out on others. Rachel never forgave her parents or her husband, and she perpetuated the abuse onto her son. She never forgave him for looking like his father.

Since Rachel was an abuser in that life, yet feeling she was always the victim, she chose this life to truly see what a real victim feels like. In the past life, she could have changed her life by choosing a better husband, forgiving everyone, and becoming the opposite of her parents. She did not take the responsibility to change in her past life, nor does she do so in this lifetime in order to help her own condition. She gave her power away here to all of the doctors and then complained about them.

In both lives, Rachel held on to old anger of being hurt and betrayed by those she trusted. She lashed out in anger at everyone else instead of releasing it in a more proper fashion. Rachel must accept responsibility for the choices and actions she made in this life, how she treated people, and what the outcomes could have been.

Rachel will probably die holding on to her anger in this life, still feeling like a victim, unless she can finally forgive all of her abusers and, most of all, herself.

Victimization

Breast Cancer

Eleanor is forty-two years old with breast cancer. She has had an amazing life and an amazing attitude about her breast cancer. But she did want to see why she had to go through this life with breast cancer. Her statement was, "I've had a great life, I love people, I love my work. I've been so happy, so why this?"

"Why have I been given my breast cancer, and what do I have to learn from it?"

Intention:

Let us go back to the root of the breast cancer.

Eleanor's story unfolds back in the 1940s, around World War II. She grew up as a young woman in England in a very prominent family. She was given the life of a princess and was very happy, but she wanted to give back to society. So, during World War II, she decided to help by being a nurse working with soldiers.

Eleanor was always thinking about everyone else first and putting herself last. She did this with her own family, caring for her parents and sisters, and now caring for the soldiers who were wounded in that lifetime. She was a wonderful spirit, a nurturer, and a lovely young woman.

She was about twenty-five years old when one of the wounded soldiers came in. She cared for him, and they fell in love. They got married, and she had a child right away. Both were very happy and had a wonderful life. She took care of their baby, and then more babies started coming one after the next. Again, she was very happy, but she was always care-taking.

Her husband's wounds manifested again. She was taking care of her husband, who had to work now to support her and the babies. After a time, her husband's wounds became so aggravated that he could no longer work. Eleanor returned to nursing while trying to keep up with her responsibilities as a mother and wife, again always the care-taker.

Eleanor finally reached fifty years old. For her, it had always been constant care until the children were grown and had left the home. Her husband had grown ill over the years and became weaker, so she was always taking care of him.

At fifty years old, Eleanor had a heart attack and died.

Last Thoughts:

Who will care for my children, husband, and grandchildren?

Lesson:

Self-love

Awareness and Connection:

Eleanor needed to take care of herself. She had always been a giver to everybody in that lifetime and this one. She put herself on the backburner, not taking good enough care of herself. Her lesson here is about loving herself enough to take the time to care for herself so that she, too, can have a healthy life.

Now, Eleanor understands her lesson and has been putting time and care into her own healing of breast cancer and for the healing of her life by balancing her caretaking duties. Eleanor left that lifetime feeling guilt at leaving people behind whom she felt still needed her to care for them, though, at that second, she herself was dying.

Eleanor came into this lifetime very much the same, being the caretaker for everybody. There were fewer people sick in this lifetime, but she was always trying to be the big sister and daughter, taking care of parents, siblings, husband, and her own children. Her lesson in that life was about strength, as she certainly demonstrated.

Victimization

Unloved

Clarisse came to me feeling her life was a mess; she could not work anymore due to physical illnesses. Her relationship with her husband was very unloving at this time. She felt that many of her family members were not supportive, and she felt a lack of friendships. She felt something was wrong with her.

"Something must be wrong with me."

Intention:

Let's go back to the lifetime that brought you into this life feeling so unloved and unsupported.

We regressed back to the lifetime that brought her into a life in Greece, where she was a young girl with an abusive father and a fearful mother. The mother was so fearful of the father that she never protected Clarisse. Her father would demand that she do different chores around the house not only to help him but also to help her mother.

When she turned fifteen years old, he sexually abused her and made her swear that she would not tell anybody or he would kill her mother. Feeling trapped and fearful, she did what he told her to do daily.

Finally, she reached twenty years old. Afraid nobody would marry her if they knew her secret, she stayed away from men. Her father was still abusive to her.

At twenty-five years old, she saw her father hit and beat her mother. She could take it no longer. She picked up a candlestick and hit him over the head, killing him.

She felt absolutely no remorse. They were able to throw her father's body into the ocean without anyone seeing or missing him.

She did it to save her mother, but her mother was very upset and angry with her. During that year, her mother cried all the time, blaming Clarisse.

No one else in the community knew their secret, but she carried around the shame, blame, and guilt all that time, even though her father was so abusive to her. She was happy she had killed him, but she also felt bad for her mother. Finally, she ended up jumping off the cliff herself.

Last Thoughts:

I cannot take this life any longer; nobody understands me or understands what I had to go through.

Lesson:

Speaking her voice

Clarisse held the secret of what her father had done to her. It was very important for her to be able to tell someone, especially to have her mother's support. Perhaps a different ending could have happened had she had that support and/or shared the secret with someone else.

Awareness and Connection:

Clarisse's lesson in this lifetime is to also speak her voice so that she can tell those around her that they cannot treat her that way any longer, or treat her in a way she does not want. Clarisse needed to ask for help from friends and family.

She also needed to use her voice to speak to her husband in this lifetime in order to clear up the issues that they have had together. Her relationship with him felt just as abusive and oppressive to her as her relationship with her father did in the other lifetime. Clarisse said she would speak to her husband to ask for what she needs.

We cleared the energy from that lifetime; however, she does have a few more lifetimes to release under hypnosis in order to have a happier and more fulfilled life.

Many times, there is more than one lifetime contributing to an issue we have here. If we release them all (as we did with the first), the outcome is stunning—and healing.

Victimization

Tortured Life

Paul came to me by referral from another client with a similar past as his and who had great success in healing his childhood wounds. Paul was grateful to find some tool that could help give him understanding about his "tortured life."

"My life makes no sense. I need some answers."

Intention:

Let us go back to the lifetime that brought you into this life having to go through torture and emotional, physical, and sexual abuse.

When regressed back to the stated intention, Paul went back to a lifetime in the Wild West. When he was ten years old in that life, he had parents who were verbally abusive to him. He was never "good enough" no matter what he tried to do.

When he turned fifteen years old, he left home looking for odd jobs and finally got a job working on a farm. On weekends, he would go into town and drink in the saloon.

At twenty years old, he was working on another farm, still drinking and now enjoying the women who worked in the saloon.

At twenty-five, he was living in a boarding house run by the saloon girls. He was fond of one of the girls and had developed a terrible temper.

Paul had stored up all of his anger from his parents, who had made him feel useless. He repeated the same feelings with various farm jobs. Occasionally, he would take his anger out on the saloon girls.

At thirty years old, Paul came home to find his girl in bed with another man. He was so angry that he set their room on fire and watched them scream and burn. Paul became numb to his feelings and circumstances.

The sheriff put Paul in jail and called for a hanging. Paul died by hanging, feeling only numbness.

Last Thoughts:

I was not a failure. They deserved to die for what she did to me.

Lesson:

Self-love

Awareness and Connection:

Paul never really learned his lesson. He had no regard for his life or for others' as well. He got to see that he was abused and became the abuser. He perpetuated what was done to him instead of trying to be a better person than his parents were. Paul got to see he had had choices and had made the wrong ones.

He also was able to make the connection that because he was the abuser and unremorseful at the end of his life, he came here to see what it felt like to be the victim once again. Here was an example of karmic balance.

Paul had seven lifetimes to release in order to feel free of victimization and to bring some understanding to his life. He was somewhat reluctant to do the others since it is difficult seeing oneself as the abuser. We were able to uncover some wonderful and heroic lives as well. And we were able to validate one of them.

Victimization

Pandora's Box

Lisa found herself on my doorstep wanting to stop biting her nails. Little did I know what was hiding in Pandora's box.

Lisa told me her life history, which included incest, emotionally abusive parents, lack of love, and deep self-esteem issues (never good enough). Lisa agreed to look at some of these other issues after we tackled nail biting.

"My life sucks. I'll never be happy — abuse, incest, lack of love, shame, not good enough."

Intention:

Let us go back to the root of your nail biting.

Lisa went back to a 1920s lifetime as a small, ten-year-old boy watching his mentally ill mother sitting alone in a room, waving her arms around. Louis only wanted to hold her arms down. So, to feel in control, he would put his fingers in his mouth.

At age ten, Louis was sent off to boarding school. On vacation, he awaited his father's return at home. His father drove up with a girlfriend and, not seeing Louis, ran him over.

Louis was now brain-damaged and at the level of a five-year-old, where he remained for the rest of his life. He was sent to a psychiatric hospital, where he lived until his death.

At the hospital, a monk taught him how to garden, which he enjoyed. The monk took him to a July Fourth celebration. The monk dropped Louis off there while he went to park the car. Louis went over to a young girl, and they walked off together. Out of curiosity, Louis raped the girl. She went off crying to her parents, who then created a mob to hang Louis. A sheriff rescued him in a truck and delivered him back to the hospital, where three guards tortured and killed him.

Last Thoughts:

What did I do? I need help.

Lesson:

Not to be spontaneous

Awareness and Connection:

Lisa understood her nail biting happened when she felt out of control, like Louis felt with his mother.

She also understood why she had to go through incest in this life. After seeing that she had been an abuser, she was able to forgive her abuser. She had picked him to teach her about victimization.

Lisa also identified her father as the sheriff, who was ashamed at what Louis had done. In this life, her parents have always been ashamed of her without her ever knowing why.

Lisa made many connections that have helped her feel more worthy and in control. She has mended her relationships, understanding why she chose them and her lessons in this life. She no longer felt like a victim but more like a strong woman who can do anything to which she sets her mind.

Victimization

<u>Take, Take, and Take!</u>

Molly came to see me feeling totally depleted. She said she had to take care of her mother most of her young life since her mother was constantly ill. When her mother died, she took care of her siblings and her ailing father. While doing so, she herself got one illness after the next, and no one ever stepped up to the plate to take care of her. She is now married, and her husband also has kidney issues and needs caring for while she continues with her own illnesses. Molly said she felt victimized by her family's "always taking, taking, taking from me. When will they take care of me?"

"I have had to be a caretaker my whole life, yet I keep having illnesses myself with no one to take care of me!"

Intention:

Let us go back to the life that has taken you into this life having to take care of everyone and having so many illnesses of your own.

Molly regressed back to a life as a young woman named Elmira in Rome. At ten years of age, she saw herself living in a big stone house with many servants. The father died in battle, but she remembered him as being big and scary. Her mother was quiet and very pretty. She had a younger brother, who was very strong but loving.

At seventeen, she met a boy and fell in love with him—only, he did not love her as much as she did him. He got her pregnant. Her mother was ashamed and sent her out of town to have the baby, who was then given away. Elmira's mother was angry and became very sad and withdrew, wanting nothing to do with her daughter. Two years later, her brother got in trouble and was thrown in jail.

At twenty-six, Elmira was married off by her mother in a political arrangement. There was not much love, and she stayed cool and reserved. At thirty years old, she had two children. One was a boy, so her husband was very pleased. Elmira felt a bit indifferent, like she was just going through the motions since that was what was expected of her.

By the time she was thirty-five, she had two more boys. One was rather impish and made her smile.

At forty years old, her husband, who was commander of the army, went off to sea.

A few years later, the son of whom she was so fond had an accident and hit his head on a rock, dying instantly. Both Elmira and her husband went into a depression.

Five years later, her husband was killed in battle. Elmira was more distraught than she thought she would be, regretting that they had not talked more and had more intimate moments.

At age fifty-five, Elmira married again, also an arranged political marriage. He was hard, harsh, and difficult, with an evil part of him. He was abusive and periodically tried to choke her. She stabbed him in the back and made it look like a robbery. She hated him so much.

At sixty-two, she had abdominal pains and died, probably from appendicitis. Her daughter, who had always been dutiful, was with her.

Last Thoughts:

I am afraid. I had been forced to marry and never was able to do what I wanted.

Lesson:

Self Love.

Awareness and Connection:

Molly connected with the life of Elmira, who was also a victim of a life of trouble, fear, responsibility, and loss. She could also identify with the feeling of indifference Elmira felt as she acted out the duties of wife and mother. Everything was always decided for her, whereas, in this life, Molly makes all the decisions as a caretaker. Only, in this life, that role is not appreciated by those for whom she cares, and she only gets taken advantage of. They, too, feel an entitlement that those in the past life felt, leaving her feeling empty.

Molly realized that she will not earn her family's love by trying to control it. She also realized that she should not depend on anyone else to take care of her, that it must be she who takes care of herself and controls only her future by the choices she has in this life.

Molly has since focused on her self-care, including quitting a stressful job that she took only because the money was good. Molly is now working on special projects as a consultant from home, where she can rest or meditate when she feels ill. Many of Molly's symptoms have disappeared as well since her last regression.

Victimization

Trapped

Wendy came into my office feeling depressed and trapped. She said she got married and had thought she would go out a lot with her husband and travel. Instead, she found herself with three children, enmeshed in cultural and religious standards that required her to dedicate herself to living a strict family life within many religious laws. She said she was feeling selfish and so unfulfilled.

"Life just took off, and now I feel trapped."

Intention:

Let's go back to the root of your feeling trapped right now.

I regressed Wendy back to a twenty-year-old young woman wearing a simple wool dress below her knees. She was in a large church in Rome around 1925. Wendy's father had died when she was ten years old, and she had been raised by her mother. She reported that when she was eight years old, she was traumatized by being raped in the woods by three men.

When Wendy became fifteen, her mother thought it best that she be sent to a convent. At twenty years old, she befriended a monk, looking for support from him. Instead, he was cold, distant, and cared only about the church. Wendy prayed a lot to God, asking for the right man to love and support her. Her prayers went unanswered, and she stopped believing in God.

At twenty-five years old, Wendy saw herself in a city in Switzerland. She was no longer at the convent. However, she was pregnant by a monk but decided to leave and become independent. She got a job working at a weaving factory with other women. She made many friends and was very happy.

At thirty, she had a boyfriend who ended up leaving her for another woman. At thirty-five, she had married an older wealthy man who sent her daughter to boarding school. At forty, she was living in a big house but was bored and unhappy, so she took a lover for excitement.

At fifty years old, her husband died, leaving her the big house. Her daughter came home and worked nearby. Her daughter lived with her since she was not married. Wendy enjoyed being home alone with her daughter and having occasional tea parties. At sixty-five, Wendy died from pneumonia with her daughter at her bedside.

Last Thoughts:

I wasted my life. I should have reached out more and not been so simple. I should have had more contact with people and married someone my age. We could have had more children and a normal life.

Lesson:

To be alone and learn more about self

Awareness and Connection:

Wendy understood why she now has a "normal life" with three children and religious standards. She also recognized why it felt boring and why she felt trapped. The life she has here is one she planned to fulfill from her last thoughts of more children and a "normal" life. The religion in the past life made her feel trapped, and in this life she has chosen a religious life again. This time, she can choose not to conform to the religious standards if she wants. She chose to live that way in this life; it was not forced upon her. She has freedom of choice here and can change her mind. Now that she knows where her religious connections were coming from and why, it may not be a priority anymore.

Wendy said this had also shed light on why she has such trust issues with men in this life. First, her father died in the past life, leaving her feeling abandoned as a child. Then she got raped by three men in the woods with no one to protect her. Then the monks did not give her the support she needed, as the church was their first priority. A monk got her pregnant. Finally, her boyfriend left her for another woman. If you cannot trust a man who is a monk, then what man can you trust?

Wendy had seven more sessions or past lives to clear in order to feel less trapped and more fulfilled.

Wendy felt victimized here, feeling she has had no choices and feeling stuck in her life. She felt that way in her past life, too. We must know that we do come here with a life script to work through Karma and to learn those lessons. But we also come here with freedom of choice that allows us to change our script at any given time based on our choices. If we do not like our script, we can make choices that reflect what we do want and take the steps necessary to get it.

CHAPTER EIGHT

Patterns

Do you wonder why you keep chasing your tail or coming back to the same immobility or self-destructive patterns and choices over and over?

Do you always choose emotionally unavailable people in your life? Do you keep choosing jobs that set you up for failure? The reason we cannot see our way clear is because we do not know what motivates our behavior.

This chapter explains the lessons that helped clients understand how to move out of their vicious cycles. These eight stories exemplify repeating patterns that prevented clients from leading the type of lives they had always dreamed of leading.

Patterns

Abandonment

Richard, sixty years of age, came to see me because he has been looking for a romantic, committed relationship. I began taking Richard's personal history, starting with his early relationships.

Although his parents were what he considered "loving," he had a strained relationship with his father, who did not understand him. He was somewhat close to his siblings. Friendships, however, were another matter. Any friends with whom he moved toward intimacy would suddenly abandon him. In the romantic realm, Richard's first relationship lasted for three years. When she left for college, she broke all ties without any explanation. He found this lack of communication baffling.

Coming from a rigid family, Richard had repressed his homosexuality. When he finally moved to London at age twenty-one, he was able to honor his sexuality and had one relationship after another. Each relationship ended in abandonment.

Most of his friends, however, were heterosexual. Even those friends left without explanation. He finally gave up on friendship and romance and had lived alone for the past ten years.

He came to me so that he could understand why abandonment was a pattern in his life.

"You cannot find commitment today."

Intention:

Let us go to the root of your abandonment issues.

Richard regressed to the 1500s as a twelve-year-old boy standing in a courtyard in France. We took him back to the age of ten, where he was sitting at a wooden table with his wealthy and politically connected family. He was one of five children.

Richard had no feeling of love from either of his parents. Their only concerns were power and money. They wanted Richard to find a vocation in the Church so that they could benefit from the connection. They did not care that he was not interested in religion or politics.

Richard just wanted to be allowed to enjoy his childhood, but he had no choice about the matter. His parents were demanding and powerful. Richard's siblings also backed their parents' ideas for his future.

At fifteen, Richard still had no desire to join the Church but found himself pressured into obeying his parents' wishes. By the time he was twenty, he had accepted the position as a religious/political leader.

This meant that Richard was not allowed to marry. Over the years, he had his share of mistresses to satisfy his sexual needs, without allowing himself emotional connections. He was not sure if the women who declared their love for him really loved him or loved his power.

This brought up the issue of trust. As his power increased, relationships became more distant, and his feelings became atrophied. As he grew older, he felt alone, unloved, and unfulfilled.

Richard began to have problems with his heart. As his heart condition deteriorated, he no longer wanted to live.

Just before his death, Richard summoned his entire family to his side. Being with his nieces and nephews, the children of the family, was the first moment of family joy. He died peaceful.

Last Thoughts:

Richard regretted that he had given up his dreams in order to fulfill his parents' desires. He also regretted that he had been unable to have a committed relationship. He would have preferred to have lived without the political clout of his position and to have been able to make his own choices.

Lesson:

Obedience (While he learned that lesson, it was taken to an extreme.)

Lesson in This Life:

To learn how to love

Awareness and Connection:

Richard realized his parents' choice did not allow him to live with personal, intimate connections so that he had to emotionally abandon others. He never trusted others who told him of their love, wondering if they really loved his power instead.

He carried the energy of separation, abandonment, and mistrust, creating the circumstances whereby others followed this pattern. His role, to achieve karmic balance in this life, required others to replay the roles of behavior he had had in his prior life, and he has continued to experience the pain of abandonment.

Richard has learned to choose the lovers and friends he wishes to have in this life. After releasing those negative energies, he should now be able to attract an authentic, committed relationship.

Patterns

Controlling

Sally, thirty-five, wanted to know why she had had a life of abuse. She explained her parents' disapproval about everything that she did. Her parents were so controlling that they did not allow Sally to make her own decisions.

As Sally grew older, she found that her friends never respected her, did not listen to her, and took advantage of her good nature. Date-raped at college, she avoided men until she met her husband at work.

Her husband was also controlling. As time went on, he became easily enraged and began to physically abuse her. After ending up in the hospital, Sally finally left him. She found refuge in a home for abused women and children.

She now wanted to understand this pattern of abuse that began so early in her life.

"Why would I choose people who are abusive?"

Intention:

Let us go to the lifetime that brought you into this one having to address the abuse.

Sally regressed to a life living in a harem in the Middle East. Going back to the age of ten in that life, she found herself as part of a poor family with five other siblings. Her family was so poor that they barely had food. Her father had died in a fight when Sally was two, leaving her mother alone to care for the children.

Overwhelmed, Sally's mother became abusive to her children. At fifteen, Sally was sold to a wealthy land-owner who agreed to send food and money to Sally's mother. Sally became one of the land-owner's four wives. Her beauty made Sally her husband's favorite.

But the land-owner raped her daily. If she did not comply, she would be beaten.

At twenty-five, she ran away but was found and brought back. Repeatedly raped and beaten, she finally died.

Last Thoughts:

I will finally find relief.

Lesson:

Strength and speaking her voice

Awareness and Connection:

Due to her past life of abuse resulting in death, Sally is still afraid to speak her voice in this life. She chose abuse as part of her journey again in this life to finally learn her lesson. Once she learns the lesson of "speaking her voice," the pattern of abuse will cease. Sally was able to understand the connection between these two lives: not speaking up for herself and releasing the painful cellular memories prevented her from moving forward and continued the abuse in both lifetimes.

We discussed the importance in this life of not allowing anyone to abuse her. Sally and I will be doing work around self-love and self-worthiness to help her find her voice so that she can finally end this pattern.

Patterns

Obligations and Responsibilities

Stephen came to my office during a time of major transition. He was letting go of a family business and deciding where to move and what his new career should be. He had been a healer, but after his father had become ill, he had given it up to take on his family business.

Ten years later, he finally found someone to buy the business. Stephen, who hated living in New York, wanted to find a wholesome community for his four children. Before taking over the family business, he had not been happy in his career as a healer. He had great anxiety around the responsibility and obligation to his family.

Unsure of what life would bring him, he came to me to resolve his anxiety.

"It's just too much pressure!"

Intention:

Let's go to the root of your anxiety about having to be obligated to and responsible for your family.

Stephen regressed to a life on a farm, describing what looked like a scene from "Little House on the Prairie." At ten, he saw himself around a table with his family, where he felt comfortable, warm, and loved. Asked if anything significant happened before the age of ten, he reported his mother had been attacked in their house by three men. With his father gone, seven-year-old Stephen and his siblings were left to watch, causing him to feel fearful and powerless.

At fifteen, Stephen was still helping his father on the farm. While his father was now emotionally detached from the family, his mother was overwhelmed. Stephen felt lost and wanted to run away, but he felt responsible for his younger brother and sister.

He stayed for another couple of years until he could no longer bear it. He moved to St. Louis, where he finally felt free. He attended school and became a dentist. However, this did not fulfill him.

He married an emotionally detached woman with a daughter. Again, his responsibility made him feel trapped.

At twenty-five, his wife died from an illness, leaving him to take care of two small children. Over the years, he had difficulty connecting with his children. He remained unhappy with his career as a dentist. By the time he was thirty-five, his children had left home. He never saw them again.

A few years after, he was in a wheelchair, feeble and ill, feeling no sense of purpose. By forty, he was dying. The only one present was a nurse. And he had not seen his children since the time they left.

Last Thoughts:

He was not sure he had wanted his children or the life that he had lived, realizing that, long before his children had left, he had emotionally abandoned them. All he could feel about them was indifference. He felt he never should have married but should have remained single and done whatever he had wanted.

Lesson:

Self-love, nurture self

Awareness and Connection:

Stephen always felt obligated to his family, which he never found fulfilling. He had wished for choices so that he could determine what he wanted to do. In that life, his obligations made him resentful. In this one, he continued trying to make everyone else happy by taking on obligations for his family, again leaving him fearful and unfilled with his career. However, he has found love and connectedness to his wife and children.

His anxiety is coming from his cellular memory around not being able to do what he wanted in that life, resulting in his fear about making the wrong decision as to what he wishes to do in this life.

We discussed that he should take time alone to think about what he really wants rather than what he feels he is obligated to do. We also discussed that making a choice around his desires, loving himself enough to work at something he loves, will finally clear his fears and feelings of dissatisfaction and break his pattern of always pleasing everyone else first.

Patterns

Intellectuals Are Safe

Nellie came to see me since she was frustrated that she never seemed to pick the right men in her life.

She was now married to a man with whom she thought she would have so much in common due to his intellect. She had gone for passion in the relationship prior to that with her ex-husband, but that man had left her after a four-year passionate love relationship for a married woman with two children.

Nellie felt safe marrying her present husband based on intellect. Only now, he was so into his work that he had no time or respect for his "stay-at-home wife," whom he had expected to work due to her intellect.

She found they were moving in different directions and did not know why she always seemed to make the wrong choices in relationships.

"I have always chosen the wrong relationships!"

Intention:

Let us go back to the lifetime that brought you into this life choosing emotionally unavailable men.

Nellie regressed back to 1941 in a small town somewhere in New England. Nellie grew up in that life in an educated, well-to-do family that was very prim and proper.

She first saw herself at a meal with her family. Her mother was directing her to put her napkin on her lap. She attended private schools as she grew up.

At age fifteen, Nellie saw that she had a boyfriend who was poor and from, as her parents put it, "the wrong side of the tracks." Nellie would sneak out to see him in some nearby woods. They were in love and very passionate.

When Nellie's parents found out, they sent her away to a boarding school to be properly educated in the finer things that life could offer. They wanted her to marry some fine, well-educated boy from a well-respected and wealthy family.

When we progressed to twenty years old, Nellie saw that she did marry just that. He was handsome, smart, very intellectual, and from a fine, wealthy family. The only problem was that Nellie was not passionate about or physically attracted to her husband. However, thinking that her parents must be right about her future and husband prerequisites, Nellie did marry him.

As we progressed to age thirty, Nellie was playing the dutiful role of mother and good wife. She realized that she had a pining for her first love and the passion she felt for him. Nellie remained quiet and obedient as she continued playing the role that was expected of her. Things remained the same as her husband withdrew into his books and intellectual life, pulling away from Nellie and the children.

Nellie became quite lonely and depressed after her children were grown. She would plead with her husband to travel with her or just go out dancing. He would get angry and tell her it was just frivolous play and that he had more important things to do.

Nellie finally got sick and died in her sixties.

Last Thoughts:

Nellie's last thought was that she was sorry she never got to travel or do so many things she would have enjoyed doing. She was also sad that she could never get the passion she once shared with her first love.

Lesson:

To speak her voice and demand that she get what she needed

Awareness and Connection:

Nellie realized she choose the exact same drama in this life. Again, she chose a passionate man who was confused as to his career path, not finishing college and rebelling against his family. Nellie got to feel what passion felt like during their four-year relationship. Due to their cultural differences in this life (he was Mexican, and she was not), these differences pulled them apart.

Going off to graduate school, she met her present husband, who again was intellectual and from a fine family. After the passionate one left, he felt safe to her.

Nellie started to see the same pattern emerge. I urged Nellie to speak up to her husband and demand the things she needed right away—without waiting this time. I told her not to stop nagging him until he agreed.

We discussed which fights or needs would be important for her, since we have to choose where we must take our stand. She worried that he might not listen. We discussed that she has the freedom of choice. She can choose the same kind of life she had last time, nag her husband in this life, or leave him and find the right man who will respect her and want to please her.

Since Nellie's children are little, she decided she would nag him for what she needs, speak her voice, and demand the respect she deserves. Nellie also realized that she needs to find balance between passion and intellect.

Pattern

So Many Divorces

Carol came in complaining about all the divorces she has had and all the wrong choices she has made in choosing men. She felt she could not trust herself anymore and did not know what to do to change her luck. Carol felt it must be karmic, and decided to try Past Life Regression work to find out once and for all what Karma she has been carrying regarding men.

"Men!"

Intention:

Let us go back to the life time that has brought you into this life making poor choices in men.

Carol regressed back to a lifetime where she was ten years old with a young boyfriend of ten years old as well. They were good friends and had a crush on each other. The time period seemed to be back in the 1700s. She had on a bonnet and a long, "pretty" dress. Carol's boyfriend carried her books back from school for her. He would push her on the swing at her house and hated leaving her.

As I progressed Carol to fifteen years old, she and her boyfriend, Jim, walked hand in hand, very much in love. They talked about marrying one day but would have to wait until he got back from college.

At twenty years old, Carol saw herself working at a pub in an inn. She felt lonely and missed Jim, for he was still at school. Carol never married anyone else since she knew Jim would come back for her and marry her as planned.

At twenty-five years old, Carol was still working in the pub, waiting for Jim to come home to marry her, when he came in with a young woman on his arm. Carol rushed to his side but then saw wedding rings on both of their hands. Carol screamed that he had promised to come home and marry her and that she had been waiting all those years.

Jim explained that he had not written to her since he had fallen in love with his present wife. He had assumed that she would have understood his lack of the written word.

Carol was devastated. She felt she was too old now to find a new love and would be working in the pub for the rest of her life.

Out of desperation and anger, she ended up marrying a man who came to the pub often and flirted with all the ladies in order to "show Jim." Carol was very unhappy with her husband since he continued to flirt with the ladies.

Jim seemed so happy with his new wife, but every day, Carol hoped he would leave her and realize it was Carol whom he truly loved. However, this did not happen.

Ten years later, Carol was in bed, basically dying from a broken heart.

Last Thoughts:

I will never find a man like Jim to love again.

Lesson:

Truth

Awareness and Connection:

Carol looked at me with her eyes wide open when she came out of hypnosis. She said, "Oh, my God. Look what I said when I died! I have never found a man like Jim to love in this life!"

I discussed with her that our last thoughts are the most important part of our life. They can bring us into a whole new life drama, part of one, a physical illness, or create Karma we have to clear. We discussed how important it would be to find a true love in this life like the one she had with Jim.

We released the sadness around her last thoughts to clear that energy. Those thoughts created energy of attracting men who were not trustworthy, like Jim. That is why they were always the wrong men.

Carol felt more confident that she could now find that man who could give her the real kind of love she wanted. She also knew to listen for hints or synchronicities that might be warning her that the man she was choosing might not be available and that he was true to his word.

Carol felt she was much smarter in this life and would be able to choose wisely now that she understood.

Patterns

They're All Wrong

Hannah came to see me, unhappy that her children had not been in touch with her and that she no longer had any friends. One by one, they seemed to disappear over time. She did not understand why everyone had abandoned her. "What was wrong with them?" It could not have been her, since she felt she was the perfect mother and friend. It seemed to be a pattern for her.

"What is wrong with them? I am perfect."

Intention:

Let us go back to the life that brought you into this life to experience the pattern of abandonment from your children and friends.

Hannah regressed back to a life in a palatial home in a country that felt like Germany. She was a small child of eight years old dressed in heavy clothes made with velvet and many underskirts. She saw herself having her hair braided by a servant. But she felt impatient and angry that she could not be left alone to play as she wished.

As we progressed, Hannah saw her mother (who was her daughter in this life) sewing in the parlor room. The mother was warm and loving but firm about what was expected of Hannah in her role. Hannah's father was very busy and had no time to spend with her except at supper.

Hannah was an only child and very spoiled. She would only listen to her mother when she got her way, so she would manipulate her mother into doing what she wanted. Every task had a condition tied to it or Hannah would not comply.

Hannah managed to use the same tactics on her father, but he only complied when it was to his benefit as well.

As Hannah progressed to fifteen years old, she saw herself looking for a husband whom she could manipulate like she did her parents. All the men her father brought to her were not good enough; however, she finally chose one out of duty.

As we progressed, Hannah tried to use her manipulation techniques on her new husband, Zoff. However, he did not have the same tolerance for them as her parents, so he only let her use those tactics for the first month of their marriage.

Zoff was Hannah's second daughter in her present life. He had a bad temper, and every time she would try to manipulate him, he would lock her in her room without dinner. Hannah would become more desperate to get what she wanted, so she would fight with him and argue why he needed to give her what she wanted. After five years of battles and being childless, Zoff had enough of Hannah and left her for good.

Hannah only had her servants to order around and manipulate in order to get what she wanted. Due to their lot in life, they had to comply. A few of them did run away since she became so very angry.

When Hannah reached forty years old, she became very sick. Alone all of those years except for her few remaining servants, Hannah had no one to comfort her. She had pushed everyone away with her manipulation and bad temper. Yet she could not understand why she had such a lonely life.

Hannah died alone and very sad.

Last Thoughts:

I have all of this wealth and yet no one. How could this have happened to me?

Lesson:

Unconditional love

Awareness and Connection:

Hannah came into this life with the same manipulation techniques that she used in that past life. Only, here, Hannah managed to use guilt to get her children and friends to do what she wanted them to do.

The mother and husband were her children here. They, too, had cellular memories of those tactics; only this time they had no tolerance for them and distanced themselves for their own protection as soon as they were able. Hannah told me they felt huge resentment toward her, and she did not understand why. She saw herself as the perfect mother, and they only saw the Hannah from their past life. Hannah told me that her ex-husband brainwashed them against her and that it was his fault.

Her friends were also not enjoying their relationships with her since they always had to do something for her before they would get together. Again, Hannah did not understand why they would not do these things for her; after all, she would for them—although she never had. They, too, became weary of her manipulations and pulled away.

I explained to Hannah that she needed to love and have relationships without asking for anything in return. It was her lesson.

Hannah is now sick in this life and is using her illness to try to get back her children and friends. She still has not learned her lesson here, and I am not sure she will. I hope one day, on spirit side, that she will finally understand that love is unconditional, for she was unable to integrate this information in this life.

Patterns

<u>The Best</u>

Jayson came to see me since he had developed an ulcer from "stress." He explained that he always had to be the best at everything. It affected his performance in sports, relationships, school, and now business. Always having to be the best at everything caused so much stress in Jayson's life that he felt he could no longer keep up with himself.

Jayson explained that he emigrated here from Russia when he was a small boy of eight, not speaking a word of English. He was put in a class for slow learners since they had no one to work with him who spoke Russian. Even though Jayson did not speak English, he sure understood that they thought he was "stupid."

In defiance, Jayson picked up the language and sports very quickly. Before long, he was put into not only a normal class but also a gifted class. He did his homework until all hours of the night to make sure it was the best, to prove to the teachers (and to himself) that he was really very smart. He did the same with sports and everything else he tried to master.

"I have to do better. I have to be the best!"

Intention:

Let us go back to the root of your needing to be the best.

Jayson regressed back to Ancient Egypt, where he was a slave working on the pyramids. He was the prize of the pharaoh since he was so very strong and worked so very fast. When Jayson was a boy in that life, he had to compete with his strong brothers to get more food to eat since strength was a gift to families and the pharaoh, and the pharaoh would gift him with food and rewards.

Jayson hated being hungry all the time, so he sought to build his small muscles and work at record speeds. As Jayson grew up, his strength and speed were used in building homes for villagers. They all wanted him, since they knew he would have their homes completed in record times.

The pharaoh finally found out about Jayson and ordered that he be in his first line of slaves to work on the pyramids. As fast and strong as he was, the guards would whip him to work even harder and faster. The more he performed, the more they would want.

At age forty, Jayson collapsed under the hot sun. The guards ordered him up and said that if he would not get up and continue, he would be put to death.

Jayson had no will to live anymore since he could not keep up with the demands made on him. It was futile to even try. Jayson was killed by a sword that went right into his gut.

Last Thoughts:

Best was never good enough.

Lesson:

Self-love

Awareness and Connection:

Jayson saw how his same drama played out again in this life. He always had to perform to survive. This time, it was not a guard killing him but his own body remembering a need to be the best in order to survive. His ulcer in this life was in his "gut," where he was wounded and killed in that Egyptian life.

We released his fear around survival and needing to be the best. Jayson was now more relaxed, understanding why he was always so driven. The intense need to be the best subsided right after the regression. He has treated his ulcer with medication and is sure it will never come back again—at least not from his stress from having to be the best. He has also taken up yoga and meditation.

Patterns

Jobs

Douglas came in with a sad look on his face and seemed very depleted. He sat down with heaviness, even though he was quite slender. He shared that he had been out of a job for the last year, and even with all of his efforts, he could not even get a dishwashing job.

Douglas had been an executive at a large company but for only two years. Before that, he had been out of work for seven years while his wife worked full-time for an insurance company. He had been a stay-at-home dad, welcoming the unemployment checks and caring for his children. Historically, he never kept a job at any given company longer than two years.

Doug told me his wife was always furious at him for not trying hard enough to get a job. This pattern of unemployment had put his marriage in jeopardy since his wife was threatening to leave him if he did not get something soon.

"Douglas is still out of a job."

Intention:

Let us go to the root of the pattern you have been experiencing with unemployment.

Douglas regressed back to a lifetime in England around 1782. He saw himself as a small boy living in a wealthy home with lots of servants. When I asked him to find his mother and father, he said they were not there. They were always away, traveling to Paris or Germany. He would be left with his tutor and servants. He always felt lonely since he was an only child.

When Douglas progressed to fifteen years old, his father had him sit with men from his printing company in order to learn the business his father wanted him to take over someday. Douglas not only hated the printing business, but he hated how it took his father away from him. Douglas tried to learn the business only to win his father's affections and the ability to get closer to him.

However, his father would leave his son's education to other employees and disappear on further travels. Douglas still felt lonely.

At twenty years old, Douglas married, hoping to finally receive the love and attention he never got from his father or mother. At first, it was all for which he had hoped. After a while, his wife would ask Douglas to get involved with his father's business or a hobby since he was at home too much and demanding her attention all the time. He tried to work at his father's business but only wanted to be at home with a loving wife. After several months, Douglas had to leave work so he could spend some time with his wife again.

We progressed to age twenty-five, where Douglas had just had a new baby. They were very happy with this new love in their lives. Again, Douglas's wife pleaded with him to go back to work so as to give mom and baby some time alone together. He reluctantly agreed but would pine away for time to be with his family at home. He could not understand why his wife needed this time or why she would not want him around. That was all he had wanted as a young boy.

As we progressed to age thirty-five, Douglas now had two children and was only wanting to spend time with them so they would not feel lonely like he had as a child. Douglas's wife continued to urge him to go to work so that they would all have room to develop as they needed. Douglas refused.

Many months later, Douglas had gone to work one day, and his wife took the opportunity to leave, taking their children to get away from their obsessive father/husband. Douglas was devastated.

For years, Douglas tried to find them and left his company in other employees' hands. He only cared about being with his family.

At age forty, Douglas was run over by a horse and carriage as he crossed the road, chasing a family he thought was his own.

Last Thoughts:

I need to be with my children.

Lesson:

Forgiveness

Awareness and Connection:

Douglas and I discussed why work brought up fears and disgust. Jobs represented losing his father and mother to work and travel. It was the block in his life that also took him away from his children and wife. He also lost his family while at work. He realized that was why work was always a negative part of this life. He did not want to lose his family again. Nothing in this life was going to take him away from his children again. His wife's anger at why he did not work was a cellular memory of the wife who wanted him to work in the past life.

Douglas felt relieved that he finally understood why he hated work so much. He discussed this regression with his wife, who compassionately understood. In her agreement to let him be at home this time with the children, he was able to see clearly the financial burden his wife has had to carry alone.

Douglas released his fear of work and losing his family and got a job two weeks later. He is still able to come home early since he is working in a school. This allows him to be at home with his children, feel a sense of self-worth, and help his wife make money to pay their bills.

Douglas was also able to forgive his father in the past life, his wife and children in that life, as well as himself for being so needy.

CHAPTER NINE

Addictions

"*The meaning of the word addiction in the English lexicon varies according to context. A positive addiction is a beneficial habit, where the benefits outweigh the costs. A negative addiction is a detrimental habit, where the benefits are not worth the negative financial, physical, and mental costs.*

Our nation has become a landscape for a variety of addictions. Examples of "negative addictions" are: sexual addiction and compulsion, drug addiction (e.g., alcoholism, nicotine addiction), gambling, egomania, compulsive overeating, shopping addiction, computer addiction, pornography addiction, television addiction, etc". Most importantly, where does it begin and why do we do it? I have found that if you have an addiction in this life, it almost always comes from a past life.

This chapter will share the addictions my clients came in to work on and eventually healed. I hope you can learn from these to understand where your addictions may have their roots.

Addictions

Alcohol

Katie came to see me to work on her fears around going out socially to parties, dances, and large gatherings with friends. Katie was only seventeen years old and a beautiful girl.

"Why can't I be like all of the other seventeen-year-olds and enjoy going to parties and hanging out?"

Intention:

Let's go back to the root of your fear about going to parties, dances, and social gatherings.

Katie went back to being a young man in a life in the early 1800s in the Wild West. She lived in St. Louis at that time. She had left home at ten years old since her father had left her family as a drunk. Katie saw herself as a drifter.

She progressed to seventeen years old in Boston, where she worked on the docks and drank enormous amounts of alcohol. She then progressed to twenty-five years old, living in San Francisco, where she also worked on the docks. She always had women as one-night stands until she went to San Francisco. She worked, dated, had fun with saloon girls, and the only desire unfulfilled was to travel abroad. Katie had fallen in love with a saloon girl who danced in many shows. When the saloon girl left for another man, Katie left for Paris.

For all of those years, Katie was a drunk and a drifter who had no real ties. She continued to be with many women and continued her drinking. She became much like her father, who left her as a small child and whom she hated.

In Paris, she painted and tried to become a famous artist but ended up dying in the south of France from alcohol poisoning.

Last Thoughts:

I die alone. Fitting.

Lesson:

Trust

Awareness and Connection:

Katie was saddened by this drifter's lifetime. She was able to see that she was abandoned and betrayed as a child by her father in that life, then by her girlfriend in San Francisco, then by the artist community in Paris, and finally by her best friend, alcohol, that finally did her in. Katie left that life feeling deep trust issues and coming into this life especially fearful around friends who were connected to alcohol or drugs. Her cellular memory remembered that people can hurt you and alcohol can kill you.

Once Katie was able to see where her fears had come from, she no longer feared friends or alcohol. She ended up having a great time in college, indulging in both.

Katie also understood why she was uncomfortable being alone.

Addictions

<u>Raging</u>

Adele came to see me since she had an abusive husband and an abusive father, who were both raging alcoholics. She was upset and confused why she chose a husband who was just like her father. She had grown to hate them both. She wanted to know what she was supposed to learn from them.

"When will he learn he can't hurt us anymore?"

Intention:

Let us go back to the life that brought you into this life with abusive, alcoholic men.

Adele went back to a lifetime in the medieval days. She saw herself waiting on men in her father's tavern when she was twelve years old. She was a pretty girl, so the townsmen would grab at her and call her names that offended her. She would run to her father for protection, but he just laughed and told her to keep serving the men. Adele's father would always drink with the men to encourage their patronage. One evening when Adele was fifteen years old, her father was drunk, and after everyone had left, he cornered her and had his way with her. As Adele cried and screamed, he would beat her until she stopped. This behavior went on for two years. Adele's father in that life was her husband in this life.

When Adele reached seventeen years old, a newcomer to the tavern saw how rough the men and Adele's father were, so he offered her a ride out of town and to a new life.

Adele was so happy to be able to escape that she agreed, even though she did not know this man. The man was kind at first, but as they got further out of the city, he, too, cornered Adele and raped her. This man was her father in this life. He left Adele by the roadside, thinking she would die there, but Adele managed to crawl to the nearest house. A kind woman took her in and healed her back to health. This woman was Adele's daughter in this life. Adele was asked to stay and keep this widow company and help her with her chores. Adele agreed as long as she would be safe from men.

Adele lived happily with this woman for the rest of her life. They helped each other and took great care of each other.

Adele died at fifty-six years old of lung problems with her lovely friend by her side.

Last Thoughts:

They can't hurt me anymore.

Lesson:

Self-respect

Awareness and Connection:

Adele understood right away why she had to come back with her abusers. She had lost self-respect by staying for so long with the alcoholic abusers in the tavern, with her alcoholic father, and finally with her savior. In this life, she needed to stay away from bars and places that involved alcohol and to not allow any man to abuse her in any way. The first sign of abuse must be her walking papers. Adele's cellular memory made her feel that she didn't deserve anything better here since she was ashamed of what happened to her in her past and present lives.

Adele feels stronger now and able to carry her integrity and self-esteem into the future, forbidding anyone to ever abuse her again. The men never learned their lessons since they carried over the alcoholism and abuse into this life. Addictions are hard to leave behind.

Addictions

<u>Pills</u>

Peter came to see me since he had been taking pain pills and anti-depressants to take away the pain of losing his wife to cancer. He loved Amy very much and could not bear the deep pain her death left in his own body. The doctors were very happy to give him anything he wanted since they knew he was so depressed. Peter almost died from accidentally overdosing on his pills.

Peter got help at a rehab but knew there were deeper issues. He asked if my work could help him with his addictions. I explained that most of our addictions come from a past life and that removing the energy from the past could help him in the present.

I also explained he could find out why he had to walk through his wife's cancer: what life brought them here together to walk through this Karma. Peter was up for both.

"I am always in pain."

Intention:

Let us go to the root of your pill addiction.

Peter regressed back to a life in Ireland during the famine. He saw himself in rags and his family painfully thin and dirty. He would go out daily, digging up roots or, if lucky, potatoes. Some days he found none, and everyone would go to bed hungry. Peter was the oldest of four boys. He was ten years old when we first came in.

At fifteen years old, Peter saw that he was the only child left since his brothers had died of hunger and malnutrition. Peter had gone out further and further to find roots and potatoes. About six miles from his home, Peter found an old bottle of whiskey a neighbor had thrown away, and that was his introduction to alcohol.

Peter's mom was very sick and dying in bed. He tried to feed her the last root he had, but she died anyway. Peter felt very guilty that he could not even save his own mother. His father had left the family when Peter was very young to look for better land.

At twenty years old, Peter was now alone. He had been drinking whisky over the years to hide his pain of loss. At twenty-three, Peter died alone with only his whiskey.

Last Thoughts:

I can't take it anymore.

Lesson:

Strength

Awareness and Connection:

Peter cried when I gently brought him back. He said he felt so bad for the poor boy in the story. I explained it was him, and he said that was why it was so sad.

Peter had tried so hard to keep everyone alive, as he had with his wife, Amy. Peter knew he would fail but did not know quite what to do. He did not want to fail again but did. Peter stayed strong in order to take care of everyone, and he did his best to take care of himself until he could no longer do so. The alcohol was a great help to endure the pain and problems in his previous life. In this life, Peter once again turned to drugs to help endure the pain of loss. He could not take the loss of Amy, as he had lost so many others from the past life. There, his drug was alcohol, and here it has been pills.

Peter felt "lighter" when he finished his regression. He said he felt he had just let go of the weight of loss he has been carrying around for lifetimes.

There were six more lifetimes we needed to release in order to clear his addictive patterns. We are still working on them and only have three more to do.

Addictions

Porn

Greg came to my office turning varied shades of red. It was really hard for him to come and admit his addiction to me. He needed to watch porn all the time, and it was finally getting in the way of his marriage. I explained that I never judge since I know it is always about lessons we need to learn and Karma we need to clear.

He wanted to stop since his wife was fed up that they could not have sex anymore without first watching porn. If he could not watch porn while having sex, he admitted to preferring masturbation. He needed my help to understand why this was so important to him.

"I am ashamed that I have a porn addiction."

Intention:

Let us go back to the root of your porn addiction.

Greg went back to the Spanish Inquisition, where his job was torturing young Jewish women before putting them to death.

Greg was twenty years old and would get sexually aroused when he tortured the women. He would then have sex with them before putting them to death. He would feel bad having to kill them but had to follow orders or he, too, would be put to death.

At age twenty-five, Greg married a lovely, very prim, and proper woman. She had no idea what he had to do in the past and was horrified every time they had sex, for he would practically rape her each time. Greg knew of no other way to have sex since that was what he was used to.

At age thirty, he had two children with his wife, but she avoided him whenever she could. At thirty-five, Greg's wife left him, taking the children with her and running off.

Greg went searching for other women (not his wife), so he could continue to have his sexual fantasies expressed.

Greg died alone at age forty-five of a disease that hit his village.

Last Thoughts:

I so enjoyed the early days [referring to his sexual romps with the women after he tortured them].

Lesson:

Love

Awareness and Connection:

Greg was a bit embarrassed when he came around. I explained that we have all been the abuser and have all been the abused. That is how we learn what we need to learn.

He also now understood why porn was so important to him here. Greg had never learned how to be intimate with a woman in a loving and gentle way. His initiation into sex was through torture and abuse.

In this life, Greg carried his cellular memory of getting aroused with the old methods he remembered. In this life, he was supposed to learn love. Greg understood this and said he would work with a sex therapist to help him and his wife attain and learn intimacy in building their sex life.

Addictions

Sex

Lulu came to see me since she was worried that she might test positive for AIDS. She was waiting for the results and felt that she had no control over her desire to be with men sexually. She admitted that she had up to ten men in one day. Now, she was frightened since she might have risked her health when one or more of the men's protection broke. She needed to know why she was so addicted to sex.

"I just can't get enough!"

Intention:

Let us go back to the root of your sex addiction.

Lulu went back to a slave lifetime in Egypt. As a child of twelve years old, she was sold to a high-ranking politician who had many wives. She knew right from the start that her life depended on pleasing her owner. She would try to do whatever was expected of her and was well-accepted. Lulu became a teenager and wanted her owner to love her the most. She would do whatever it took to please him.

At twenty years old, she demanded to be the first wife since she loved and pleased the owner the most. He became impatient with her and threatened her that he would share her among the other politicians if she did not behave. Lulu thought he was only teasing her, and she began to nag him.

Finally the owner called her bluff and sent her away to the others. Lulu was frightened since she thought the owner had loved her. She felt very vulnerable and afraid that if she did not please all of the politicians, she would be put to death. She performed her best with each one to fight for her life. They all liked her and kept her very busy. Lulu enjoyed the attention and took it as love.

At age forty, she started to get tired and looked older. The men stopped asking for her since they, too, were getting older. At age fifty, Lulu was no longer needed and finally put to death.

Last Thoughts:

I thought they loved me!

Lesson:

Self-love

Awareness and Connection:

Lulu was sad as she looked back on that life and recognized the similar drama in this life. She was always trying to please those she slept with so that they would love her. Her cellular memory would make her feel that if she did not sleep with a lot of men and please them, she would be put to death. This fear made her want to sleep with a lot of men to cover her bases and made her want to please them all.

This time, she would be put to death because of pleasing so many of them and for not loving herself. It was time for her to look within for approval and love and not worry about others. She would be her own best advocate.

We released the energy tied to the need to be loved and pleasing others, and Lulu felt there was much less need. She also wanted to go forward, stepping into her self-respect and loving herself enough to want to please only herself. We await her test results.

Addictions

Smoking

Loren came to me to stop smoking. She hated the dirtiness of the habit: the yellowing of her teeth, the nicotine-stained fingers, and everything she owned always smelling like smoke. Loren had only been smoking for six years, starting in her senior year of high school. She told me she had never thought she would smoke, but, due to peer pressure, she would smoke only with her friends on weekends. Before she knew it, she was addicted. To break the habit, she tried many things that did not work, like patches, fake cigarettes, and gum chewing. She smokes the most when with friends and drinking alcohol.

"I hate this dirty habit, but I just can't stop!"

Intention:

Let us go back to the root of your addiction to cigarettes.

Loren regressed back to a lifetime in the Wild West. She saw herself as a young boy in loose trousers and a hat. She said she looked about twelve years old and was called Samuel.

Loren saw herself helping her dad on their farm. Her dad was her dad in this life, a hard worker and a quiet man.

When I asked her to describe her mother, she cringed. She said her mother was a "bitch." She also said her mother was her mother in this life. Her mother would nag her and her father all day. Nothing they did was good enough, and she would order them around like slaves. Samuel's father would just cower and clam up. Samuel lost respect for his father for not standing up for himself but understood how his mother could take away one's energy and power.

Samuel decided to leave home at age sixteen to get away from his nagging mother. He felt guilty leaving his father behind with her but could not make him go with him when he left.

Samuel drifted from town to town. He picked up work wherever he could find it, doing chores for people on their farms. He also went into town to drink since he did not have anything else to do. He liked the saloon girls and cigarettes while he would drink. He never wanted to marry since he did not want a wife like his mother. His addictions to saloon girls, cigarettes, and alcohol became his life after a hard day on the farms.

When Samuel was thirty years old, he had one of his drunken stupors. The saloon girls were fed up with him since he would usually pass out from the alcohol before being with them. They left him to sleep it off once again, and when they returned, they found him dead. He had choked on his vomit while sleeping in bed. Samuel had never awakened before he died.

Last Thoughts:

None

Lesson:

Worthiness

Awareness and Connection:

I helped Loren release her feelings of unworthiness from her mother, farmers, and the saloon people. She was able to make the connection that her mother and father in this life were those in her past life. She felt unworthy growing up in this life as well.

She also saw how she used substances to make her pain go away, which she does here, too. The substances were her only joy in the past life and giving up smoking here made her feel she would have to give up joy once again.

She also understood why she had such a love-hate relationship with her substances and why she enjoyed them in the same environments with friends and alcohol. Even though she found joy with them, they ended up killing her.

Loren did not want to die once again from her addictive behaviors.

Before Loren came out of hypnosis, I gave her subconscious suggestions of not wanting those addictions anymore, that she would actually find them repulsive.

Loren left the office feeling disgust for cigarettes and threw out her pack on her way out.

(I usually do several steps for smoking and eating issues. I use several techniques that reframe, desensitize, and consciously provide understanding to replace the habit with a productive situation. I also use hypnosis to finally give the subconscious the appropriate suggestions, as I did with Loren. Loren never needed the other techniques; the regression was enough.)

Addictions

Gambling

Barry came to me to see why he was having such a hard time staying away from the casinos. He explained that he came from a financially comfortable family but always worried they would lose it and that one day he would have nothing. Since childhood, he has obsessed about making money. He had the first newspaper route, started investing money in his teens, worked two jobs at the same time, and played cards in high school and won often. In college, he bet on the football games and won bigger sums of money. In his last year in college, he went to Las Vegas for a bachelor party and got hooked on a fast money-making track. He won big but never walked away when he was losing. Barry was always up and down.

He finally met a lovely woman who worked in the stock exchange, and he felt he found a gold mine. He did fall in love with her and married her but now fights with her all the time about his gambling. She has threatened to leave him if he does not stop. I asked Barry if he really wanted to stop, and he admitted that he did not. I explained that by going into a regression that would find the root of his gambling, we could let go of the obsessive energy around it. He was up for the challenge.

"I have to gamble; it is the only way I can really make money."

Intention:

Let us go to the root of your gambling addiction.

Barry regressed back to a lifetime in Paris during the turn of the century. He was born into a wealthy family that offered everything anyone could want. Barry was not allowed to play with other children unless they were cousins or from other wealthy families. Since both were not too available, Barry found himself alone a lot as a child. Barry loved to paint and was quite good for a child. He painted landscapes that he fantasized about and still-life that he found in his home.

When Barry was fifteen, his parents were killed in a horse and buggy accident. Barry was left all of his family's wealth, but he was very depressed. He had no one with whom to share it. Barry was awkward since he never spent much time with other children. As he went out to meet other teens, he would be made fun of or ripped off by those who only wanted his money. Barry poured himself into his paintings even more.

They were actually quite good. He tried to get attention for his painting, but the market was flooded with other painters who were even better. Barry tried using his money to buy critics' approval, but it did not get him very far.

Barry felt he needed to hide his wealth to be accepted into the art community since most of the artists were starving and poor. He started giving away his money at age twenty-five to many charities. By age thirty, he was almost poor.

By still painting, but without money, Barry felt he would finally be accepted into the artist community. He took a chance by giving the rest of his money away and headed for the streets and pubs of Paris, where his art colleagues resided. His awkwardness still kept most artists at a distance. Barry got to see that it was not his money that turned them off but his personality.

Now that Barry had no more money, he did not know what to do. He started drinking and, by age forty, died on the streets in Paris in rags, with his paintings in hand and starving to death.

Last Thoughts:

I should never have given my money away for acceptance. It never worked, and now I am dying because of it.

Lesson:

Strength

Awareness and Connection:

Barry never trusted his financial comfort in this life since, in the past life, his parents died and everything changed, including his financial status. Barry realized that he loved being with friends in this life, and part of his money pursuits actually put him with people who liked him and his ambition. In the last life, he could not make any friends.

Barry also realized that gambling made him feel alive, whereas money in the past life made him feel dead and alone. Giving up the money in the last life killed him, so if he stopped gambling (where he made money in this life), that would kill him as well — or at least his cellular memory or subconscious believed that.

Barry's wife disapproved of his gambling and of his addiction to it. She always put him down at whatever he did. Barry saw her love as conditional, like his artist friends from Paris. He felt he needed to take a better look at why he married her: financial security versus love. Once again, money could ruin his life unless he could find balance.

I helped Barry release his fear of giving up gambling, equating it with his poverty and death from his past life. We discussed that finding a good job would provide for him, and finding friends and love in his life would provide the balance for which he was searching.

Addictions

Shopping

Donna came to see me to stop her shopping addiction. She loved to shop for everything: clothes, furniture, food, and anything else she could buy. She loved to shop and spent any money she or her husband made, always leaving them short at the end of the month. Her husband has put down his foot and said, "No more!"

"I get such a high from shopping."

Intention:

Donna regressed back to a young girl in Ireland. She was very poor and ate raw potatoes. Her parents tried to farm their land but had mostly rocks and dry soil.

Donna had three sisters younger than she. Her dad was depressed since he was hoping for sons to help on the farm. Donna saw her parents as her sister and brother in this life. Her siblings there were her nieces and nephews in this life.

At age fifteen, Donna went to Dublin since it was the nearest city to get a job and make some money. She got a job as a maid for a wealthy family. They never let her get close to their children or them and only wanted her to clean and keep house. For years, she worked hard and sent her money home for her family. The family she was working for paid her very little for all the hard work she did.

At age twenty, Donna found out that her family all got sick and died. She was devastated since she loved them very much.

At thirty years old, Donna was let go since the couple was moving to England, where they sent their children for their schooling.

Donna did not know where to go or what to do but had saved some money since her family had died. She rented a room in a boarding house. Donna spent some days walking in the city, looking into the store windows at all of the beautiful clothes, candies, and furniture. She dreamed about having them all, but, of course, she could not have any.

Later that year, she ran out of money. Donna felt so alone and so poor once again. She could no longer pay for her room so had to go out onto the streets. She would try to warm up by fires in the oil cans in the streets and beg for food. Donna finally died from pneumonia with no one around her.

Last Thoughts:

I came into this world with nothing, and I leave with nothing. I am ready to go.

Lesson:

Strength

Awareness and Connection:

Donna had no problem understanding why she felt so good shopping all the time. She was making up for lost time. She had nothing in that life, so she needed "everything" in this one.

Donna also connected that she hates cleaning in this life, and shopping would get her out of her house so she did not have to clean. Donna laughed when she realized how much she hates potatoes in this life, as well.

Donna loves her sister and brother in this life. They mean everything to her. She was happy to see that she was able to come back with them and have more time with them. She adores her nieces and nephews, too.

Donna was so amazed at the past life and how it made so much sense in this one.

I explained that after releasing the sadness around her family's death, her poverty, and starving that she could now feel less obsessed about filling a sadness or void in her life here.

We also released her fantasy about all that she saw in the windows of Dublin and jealousy of those who could afford them. That, too, helped take away the strong need to have it all.

Donna called to let me know it worked! She was no longer interested in shopping so much and having everything. She admitted that she still liked to pick up an occasional sweater or baked good.

CHAPTER TEN

Glossary and Capabilities—Through the Eyes of Past Life Regression

Past Life Regression's Profound Healing Capabilities

Speed

Past Life Regression therapy goes right to the root of an issue, phobia, trauma, relationship, etc., therefore expediting the healing process. In the same session, the negative emotions that arise are released from the lifetime immediately through breath work. Again in the same session, a spiritual guide is summoned to help answer all of the "why" questions, our lessons from the past and the present, and any other questions that might help us understand this life better.

Also in the same session, we understand the Karma and relationship connections to the present life, allowing us to make "choices," hopefully the right choices that can finally shift the past Karma we have been carrying.

After one session, many people are healed from issues that may have plagued them for many years. Sometimes more than one session is necessary if information given to us by our guides indicates more than one lifetime is involved. We may have to work through multiple past lives in order to release the energy that may be causing the issue.

Releasing Negative Emotions

When we experience trauma, fear, anger, loneliness, or any other negative emotion, my theory is that our subconscious takes a deep breath in and holds that emotion, storing it in the body, memory, or in our energy field. We call this an energetic block.

We then carry that negative emotional blockage through life and into the following lifetimes until it can be released. It is very important to release these emotions since emotions cause illness. We have witnessed incredible changes in the physical body after releasing these emotions. Those who have illnesses due to these negative emotions have actually been healed.

For example, a woman who has asthma in this life found she died in a fire in a past life, choking on the smoke. After we released the fear she had during that death, she awoke without a trace of asthma. Releasing this fear also released the phobia of fire she has had her entire life. She remains cautious, but the intense fear of fire is no longer present.

We actually feel physiologically lighter, since the burden of carrying the heavy emotional blockage through life is gone.

Understanding the "Why" Question

Our nature as human beings is to ask the question *"why?"* We have an innate need to understand life and how it works. When we are children, we ask why the sky is blue, why we have certain body parts, why you had to have that little sister. As we grow, our need to know does not change.

This is especially true when we experience a painful event. We often ask, "Why did … have to happen to me?" "Why did I have to have such a … mother or father?" "Why do I have such a crazy phobia when nothing ever happened in this life to cause it?" "Why was I born an orphan?" "Why does everything seem to go wrong in my life?" These are just a few of the why questions that we feel we *need* to know and can find out from our regression.

Past Life Regression helps us understand all of these questions and more. We frame our intent or question for the subconscious as a why question. For example, "Let us go back to the life that brought you into this life to be with a certain relationship, go through a certain trauma, etc."

Going through the regression, we will see many of the same people who are in our present lives, in many similar dramas or traumas that we experience here.

If our *why* questions are not answered in the regression, we then have another opportunity to have them answered on the "spiritual side," using a guardian angel, spiritual guide, the light, or even your higher self.

Once we have satisfied the *why* questions, we can then make the connection with this life and use the information to once again lighten our burden and move forward in life, understanding the reasons we chose what we chose.

We also learn a lesson from that time, as well, that we could also put into effect to make changes in this life. The answer to our *why* question may be the final puzzle piece we have been searching for in this life during years of traditional psychotherapy. There is a sense of peace when we make peace with the *why* question that went unresolved before.

Karma (Cause and Effect)

Many people misunderstand how Karma works. Most feel that if they are having a bad life or situation, they must have done something terrible in a past life.

It does not always work that way. Sometimes, we have a victim life over and over in order to learn a lesson of "speaking our voice." We choose such a life in order to push ourselves into speaking up for ourselves since we possibly did not learn to do so or could not do so in past lifetimes due to circumstances.

Another example would be killing someone in a past lifetime and then healing him or her in another. Karma can take many forms, and it is you who decides how you create your drama in the next life in order to learn your lesson(s) in the best possible way with the best-selected soul group.

One usually chooses the people with whom one has "unfinished business" so that one can finally complete the Karma or change it by our choices. All of the stories are filled with lessons, and the people are the vehicles who teach the lessons or allow the lessons to be taught.

In doing Past Life Regressions, one finds out what one's Karma is with certain people and events. One can finally change one's Karma by satisfying the reason we chose this Karma on the other side. With Karma, one has freedom of choice. One does not have to satisfy one's karmic ties here. One can wait to do this in another lifetime or on the spiritual side. There is no right or wrong; it just is. We will reap what we sow in some way.

Life Lessons—Past and Present

One comes to this earth for three things: to love, to be loved, to learn lessons, and to clear Karma. There is nothing one goes through in life from which one cannot learn a lesson. When one experiences a wonderful moment admiring nature, for example, one could be learning how to appreciate life's naturally made surroundings or how to be in the moment. If one has a trauma, one could ask why this happened, or one could ask what was needed to be learned from this event.

If one could learn something from any situation and use it to enhance this life then the pain of the event does not seem as bad. Lessons are abundant.

The following are some lessons my clients have shared: love, strength, compassion, speaking one's voice, living life each moment, never taking a life, truth, trust, duty, loyalty, honesty, self-love, and patience.

We learn our lessons so they do not repeat themselves. Sometimes we create the same dramas in each lifetime in order to learn the same lesson. Sometimes we create dramas that are more difficult because we did not get the lesson in the last life. Sometimes the lesson may skip lifetimes until it is needed for a certain life lesson or circumstance.

We are constantly learning, but sometimes we do not realize it or get the lesson. It is why we are here. It is important to find out why you are here and what it is you need to learn so that you can accomplish it. However, there is no judgement if we don't learn our lesson. We are not "bad". We have an opportunity to learn it on the spirit side or when we come back into another life.

Why can't we learn from something easier? Well, we may have tried in past lifetimes yet never learned what we choose to learn that way. If we did not learn the necessary lesson in previous lifetimes, we may choose something more powerful that will push us into learning it this time.

When we are uncomfortable or in pain, we do not want to stay there since it does not feel good. Therefore, we change something to make ourselves feel better.

Sometimes we cannot learn something without experiencing intense pain or suffering, for other stimuli would not propel us to the lesson at hand—for example, victimization. Let us say that in this life, we were sexually abused by a family member. We walk in a numb or shameful reality until our subconscious is capable of confronting the truth and making change. When it feels too bad, we feel hopeless, depressed, fearful, or trapped, so we feel we have to make a change or die. At that point, we have choice. We can choose to speak our voice. We can say, "You cannot do this to me anymore" and stand up for ourselves. Or we can leave the abusive situation. Also, we may try to help others who have experienced the same trauma. Our other option is to perpetuate the abuse that was done to us.

When we have learned our lesson, we do not need to keep learning it again and again. There are always new lessons to learn since we are always creating new Karma with new relationships. We may need to learn the same lesson again by creating new Karma if we forget our lessons from before. We may choose a new way to learn it, depending on what created it.

If we learn what we need to learn in this life, we can go forward using this information, putting it into effect so we can complete this life's lesson and hopefully moving on to further our learning.

Everything in life is a lesson or should be. Whatever we experience, we should look at it with eyes of "What could I learn from this experience?"

Using Past Life Regression therapy, we find out what our lessons were from the past, enabling us to see if they were accomplished and, if not, why?

We also find out what our lessons are from our present life, what we are here to learn. This process will make life easier to handle, more comprehensible, fuller, and more spiritually connective.

Feeling Spiritually Connected

As mentioned before, in doing Past Life Regression, we connect to a higher universal purpose. First, we realize we incarnate, indicating there is no death, just a change of dimension, drama, lessons, and players. We get to experience ourselves both in the physical plane and then the spiritual one.

We connect to the light or to spiritual guides, guardian angels, masters, and our higher selves (our spirit or soul) in order to understand our life's lessons and other questions we would like answered. We realize and feel all of this spiritual help, guidance, and support around us, helping us feel more connected to a larger and more loving family. We feel and understand it is not God who is punitive but our own choices that create our realities.

God remains all-loving, all-caring, and all-truth, there to support and love us through our life's lessons. We realize our prayers are always heard and answered, even if not how we hoped but rather how they needed to be.

We realize that we are all God, His breath our spirit, each one of us another part of Him, therefore all of us the same. We all have different dramas only for learning. The bag lady has the same soul as the doctor, each different in lessons only. Neither is better than the other.

Many times, the bag lady has a more evolved spirit than the doctor, since she chose to come into this life humbling herself with such a difficult, painful life in order to evolve further spiritually, understanding she needed this in order to grow to the next spiritual plane.

We see that we have all been the bag lady, the doctor, the abuser, the abused, the African, the Jew, the teacher, the student, the saint, and the sinner. There is no judgment, only lessons and spiritual growth.

Learning Tolerance and Non-Judgment

We come into this world in a family unit that we have chosen for a variety of reasons. This family and their present lives start formulating our realities, the way we see the world. Again, this is for resolving Karma and learning lessons.

Our experiences can be altered by our freedom of choice. For example, we may come into this life choosing to be Jewish in order to learn about tolerance and/or judgment. Perhaps one was an SS soldier in World War II and hated the Jews for creating difficult choices whether to follow orders and kill them or die by speaking out against it. The choice was to follow orders, so this hate continued to grow. Judgment and generalizations were made about the Jews to alleviate one's own guilt, fears, and shame. Finally, the soldier dies, and on the spiritual side, he realizes all of this: how his judgment and intolerance clouded his choices due to his own negative emotions.

So, he decides to come back Jewish to help understand what that feels like and to dispel the judgment and intolerance from the last life. Again, we have all been the abuser, all been the downtrodden, all been of each religion, culture, sex, and personality. Therefore, we are all equal; no one is to blame, and no one is better or worse than anyone else. So we must let go of judgment. It is not our right to judge others — only ourselves.

We are usually our own worst critics or judges, for we subconsciously remember what that is like on the spiritual side. What we must learn is that God is all-loving, all-truth, and all-forgiving. Since we are part of God, we must be the same: all loving, all-truth, and all forgiving, both of ourselves and of others.

Once I asked why I was given such a gift in the work that I do. Why me? The answer came from a very wise woman who said that I was no better or gifted than the auto mechanic. For if it were not for his gifted abilities, he would not be able to repair my car that brings me to my client. If he were not there, I could not see my client.

We are all here with our own gifts and talents to fulfill our lessons and Karma — not because someone is either better or worse than the next.

The Essenes, the wise community that wrote the Dead Sea Scrolls, understood this in their community. The people would choose a job to help teach them what they needed to learn. A servant may have chosen that role to learn how to humble himself, for that is what his ego needed. A professor needed to practice his teaching skills. A doctor to heal some of his own wounded psyche.

The amazing thing was that they all knew they were equal, but they knew what they needed to do to work through their life's lessons and Karma. They had no egos, for humility was a way of life. Being in ego was a sin. They each knew their own divine connection, understanding each one was a part of the whole. There was never judgment, just mutual respect in the Essene community.

We have come so far, forgetting so much.

Energy

Everything in life is made up of energy. Our thoughts and emotions are energy, as well as our words and deeds. Studies have shown that when patients were hooked up to a biofeedback machine and sent loving thoughts by a person in another room, their immune systems got stronger. Later that day, one of the patients received negative thoughts, and his immune system became depressed. The reason for this is that thoughts are energy, and when we send thoughts to a person, we send either positive or negative energy.

We see that these thoughts can affect us physically, as per the receiver mentioned before. If this is true then we have to be ever so careful and responsible for all that we say and think. The power of thought and word can create physical change. We can change many things in our environment. We can literally change the world.

These manifestations happen from lifetime to lifetime as well. When a person is on their deathbed, their last thoughts are very important and affect their next lifetime. For example, if a person thinks, *I've been smothered by responsibilities my whole life,* they may reincarnate with asthma.

They also may choose another life, much the same as the last, to learn that we all have freedom of choice. We do not have to feel so responsible; that is our choice. The next time, we may choose to have a simpler life so that we do not create a smothering trauma or experience. This can shift the Karma so it does not have to be addressed again.

We are constantly creating as we are constantly thinking. If we can change things or create things by what we think, let us think about the power of love or think loving thoughts. Can we make a world that is loving, peaceful, and beautiful? Ultimately, yes. What prevents that from happening? One thing: fear. Fears of change or of the power to create. Greed, the desire to always want more, even when we have plenty. Control or power resides in the ego. Ego has to transform for our highest good.

What stimulates greed, control, and power is last lifetimes of Karma that made us this way in this life. This work can help shift those fears.

Another pattern we carry from past lifetimes is what I call "the non-deserving mode." This is when we place ourselves last, on that back burner, the place where we subconsciously feel that we do not deserve to live in a loving, peaceful, or healthy world. We can also release that negativity by doing past-life work.

Illusion versus Reality

We walk on a path that is unique to each one of us. We all have our own blueprint that is like no other in the universe. This blueprint is comprised of past-life histories as well as present-life history.

From the day we are born, we are exposed to various stimuli, from the air we breathe to how nurturing or abusive our caregivers might be. We may feel secure or depressed, feelings that may be lingering from another life or from this present one. Our mother may be kind to our brother but may feel anger toward us. Again, this may be past-life-related. You start to see the world from a sad and wounded psyche, yet your brother may be happy and well-functioning. He may be getting A's in school while you are struggling for C's. Your mom may get angry at you for not doing well in school while praising your brother. Your self-esteem is poor now, but your brother's is great. Your parents ask what is wrong with you since you do nothing right.

Are you this awful person? No, but you think so due to your "reality." All of the circumstances from birth on created obstacles that created your reality. It was your relationship with your parents in this set of circumstances that shaped your reality. Yet it was the way your parents perceived you from old karmic feelings that made them react to you in such a negative way, so, in reality, you are really fine. Only you do not think so since you are a product of their reality, the reality they created for you.

You may have been a victim in past lifetimes as well. Perhaps this reality was formulated to teach you "how to speak your voice," to stand up for yourself, not allowing even parents to put you down or be abusive to you.

Can you change this reality? Yes, you have freedom of choice and can alter this reality by fulfilling your lesson. When you confront your bother (who has been happy) to support your feelings about your parents, he refuses, saying you are crazy, that it was not like that. Your reality is but an illusion to him because his reality was experienced differently. Neither of you are wrong; you just experienced life differently, so your realities are different. What is one man's reality is the other's illusion. So, again, we cannot judge wrong from right, for they are both right. Is, therefore, everything we experience an illusion?

Physical Illness and Healing

The healing of physical illness is a common phenomenon in this work. Most of our physical illnesses are due to emotions. We see that stress, fear, anxiety, etc. can cause headaches, heart disease, arthritis, asthma, and so on. The premise is that if we "hold in" our feelings, they can manifest into illness. This holds true for this and our past life.

Is it possible to carry emotions and illnesses from lifetime to lifetime? The answer is yes. When my clients have gone back to the root of their illnesses, we release the emotions that caused their illness either from this life or a past lifetime.

Many times, we may witness a physical healing after this release. For example, an older man in his sixties came to me with rheumatoid arthritis, not being able to sit comfortably in my chair. We went back to understand his relationship with his parents. Through his tears, he reported that his father made him feel ashamed of his sensitivity about the world. We released his shame from his past and present lives. His arthritis felt significantly better. After weeks of releasing shame and fear from his past, he reported that his arthritis no longer bothered him at all.

Another client went back to a lifetime where she was smothered from smoke inhalation in a fire. As she died in that fire, we released the trauma and fear she experienced. She had had asthma since she was a small child in this life. After this release, she reported that she was symptom-free. Years later, she reported the same.

If we can heal illness by releasing emotions then we can prevent physical illness from occurring by releasing our negative emotions daily so they won't turn into illness. There are different methods we can use to do this. Contact me if you want further information .

The Power of Healing Self

We can go to the greatest healers and yet not heal. The reason for this can be that we give away our power to the healer. If our attitude is helpless or fearful, the energy is negative. Negative energy can bring down our immune system and manifest our greatest fears. If we trust in ourselves (God) that we can heal, remain positive in attitude, and visualize the illness away, we can heal ourselves. It sounds simple, and it is.

Illness is a way our body is trying to teach us something. When we get a headache, perhaps the body is trying to tell us we are straining our mind too much and need to rest it. It can be from stress or some type of overload. There are studies showing that someone else's negative energy can affect another person to whom it is directed.

Research has indicated that pleasant or positive stimuli can help heal illness. For example, there are pet hospitals for patients to play with dogs, cats, birds, and other animals while recovering from an illness. Some hospitals have plants that can be tended, comedy movies, and other positive stimuli to aid in the healing process. All these things help boost the immune system.

Our mind is a powerful tool when used properly. We can heal ourselves. Our healers are only as good as our healing attitudes. We have freedom of choice to heal or to remain ill. We must learn never to give our power away but to use it in healing ourselves.

The Power of Anger and Fear

Anger and fear are two of the most powerful and destructive emotions. As I mentioned before, we can depress someone's immune system by our thoughts and actions. We can do damage to ourselves, as well, by holding on to negative thoughts and feelings.

Anger can manifest physically, causing diseases such as cancer, ulcers, migraines, etc. It can affect the health of others around us, too. Anger does not serve anyone well, so it should be released as quickly as possible to prevent manifestation. When others experience our anger, they can internalize it and get physically sick or react to it. If they react to it, they will become either defensive or destructive. Again, neither serves wellness in anyone involved.

As with every emotion expressed, we will have to be responsible in a karmic way when we leave this earthly plane. Anger only breeds more anger, revving hatred and violence. Anger is a root of evil and a perpetuator of evil deeds. We still have wars, murders, and other evil deeds all fired by anger. Again, if anger can create all of this destruction then think what we could accomplish if we could release this emotion before it could take hold.

Fear is another destructive emotion. Fear can incapacitate us; it can drive us to act spontaneously or destructively. It, too, can manifest physically, causing illness such as ulcers, intestinal track problems, asthma, arthritis, etc.

Fear leaves us open and vulnerable to negative attachment. It closes our minds, causing intolerance and judgment. It makes us contract rather than expand, minimizing our experiences and learning. When we act out of fear, it is acting irrationally without clarity or balance. It can create ignorance. Fear also breeds more fear.

All that fear does to us, it can do to others as well. Again, we are ultimately responsible for our actions, so we face karmic repercussions. We can release this negative emotion, clearing away physical harm to others and ourselves, and create a place of reason and balance.

The Intricacy of Incarnating

People often ask how we decide when to incarnate and with whom. The information offered in channeling and with Past Life Regression work is that we develop a tapestry mixed with people with whom we have karmic debt or love, lessons that need to be learned, dramas that still need to be played out, metaphors that need to be completed, and wounds that still need to be healed.

We may choose the same culture or a different one depending on the need. The same holds with religion or color. We may need to be geographically located in a certain part of the world. We usually reincarnate with the same close people in our lives each time, depending if these people can fulfill the dramas and lessons. We see our connections to people who may be our doctors, postal workers, or healers in this life, again completing Karma from other lifetimes.

It has been said that there is a place where there are records kept that hold everything we do and say and think. After we review these records, there is something like a big computer in the sky that processes all of this information, deciding who would best help us learn the lesson we need to learn and what circumstances would best facilitate this learning. We then wait for the right moment and enter, choosing the right parents for the job. They, too, have to agree to make this work.

It makes us wonder how special, not awful, these abusive people are in our lives to choose to come here to be that way in order to help us learn our lessons. Who but someone who loves you deeply would want that awful job?

At the time of decision-making on the other side, your higher soul can clearly see that choosing a particular life may not always be joyful but may be filled with pain necessary for your greatest growth. You must applaud your soul's higher wisdom.

Spiritual Pre-Natal Care

The soul entering a new body waits for the right moment to come in. It may come and go during the nine months, testing the waters, so to speak.

During the time the soul is in the baby, the baby picks up all of the feelings and thoughts of its mother. It hears and also intuitively picks up its environment. It still remembers its past, present, and future. If a mother did not plan the pregnancy and does not want the baby, the baby feels all of these feelings. This is why we may feel unwanted growing up as a child, even if the parent changes his or her feelings. A baby in *utero* can pick up conversations between the mother and others, affecting the baby's attitude toward the other person.

It is so important to understand all of this when going through pregnancy to ensure a healthy emotional environment for the baby. At birth, the soul decides to go through with the plan and enters the body of the baby for good or decides it is not the right time or parents. This is one reason for being still-born.

When the soul decides it is not the right time, the parent is not ready, etc., the soul will withdraw and wait for another time that is more opportune. The soul of the baby goes back to the spiritual side to stay with loved ones and guides until the time is right. They may also do this as a lesson for the parents that they might have needed.

Accidental versus Deliberate Death

We all have to die in that we have to shed our physical bodies from lifetime to lifetime. Our spirit never dies as it changes its dramas and incarnations as well as its physical bodies.

Before we come to this earthly plane, we choose what way we need to leave it. It may be one of illness due to the emotions we experienced in life or it may be an accident to experience a lesson or teach one to a loved one. Sometimes, an accident may occur that we did not choose. Not everything can happen exactly as we have chosen since we all have freedom of choice here and can choose to be in a situation we were not aware of at the time of spiritual choice.

There can also be great catastrophic death from earthquakes, holocausts, airplane crashes, etc. Sometimes this exit is again for personal lessons, but sometimes it is for universal lessons. For example, the Holocaust was a universal lesson of intolerance, injustice, prejudice, insanity, and not speaking our voices. Environmental catastrophes are wake-up calls to take better care of the earth, since we are polluting, removing her natural resources, and killing off the natural food supply.

The question is: do we learn our lessons? Not usually. We must learn to listen to these calls and our own endings to learn what it is that we need to learn. The catastrophes, illnesses, and accidents will only get worse if we do not listen. Something needs to wake us up. We do not need to fear death since we truly do not die.

Energy Attachment

I will not say much on this subject since this has never been a place of comfort for me. However, that does not mean it does not exist. Spirits are energy. We are made up of energy, and, therefore, when our body dies, the energy can remain. Either this energy can go to a dimension called the astral plane (or what I call the spiritual side) or it can linger on the earthly plane.

If the death was a shock or accident and the person was not ready to go, the spirit may need time to adjust and stick around or to choose a physical form to enter to feel connected. It will choose a person who is open due to illness, depression, or cult worship since their openness allows for easy entry. We call this spirit attachment. If the attached spirit had an illness itself, it may give its new host that illness.

Just like releasing emotions, we can also release spirits. Most of them are grateful for our assistance since many feel trapped, not knowing how to leave. We send them to the light, where they belong to begin with.

Themes of Music Vibration, Water, Intuitiveness

During these regressions, certain underlying themes come out, such as music vibration. One woman came to me having been a singer in many lifetimes. When asked what significance music played for her, her answer was that singing helped her to speak her voice. It was also channeled that music is "the breath of life."

We all respond to vibrations of energy since we are all made up of these vibrations. Music is a series of vibrations that help us stay healthy and grow as well as stay connected. Sounds communicate to our soul, communicating peacefulness, joy, sensitivity, and love. As they say, "Music soothes the savage beast."

Water is another underlying theme that has come up for us to look at. I myself had a series of synchronicities with water. At age eight in this life, I had a near-death drowning experience in a pool at day camp. Very calmly, I went under, watching the children above, almost breathing, and feeling very peaceful.

I was rescued and walked away from it. Subsequently, I learned that I had committed suicide in my last life by walking into the Pacific Ocean and drowning there.

Later in this life, I had a wonderful experience with ayuverdic medicine, having massage and steam as part of the healing. In each session, they put a steam tent over my body and head. I always had to ask that they not put my head under the tent, for I felt claustrophobic and fearful of the mist from the steam.

One day, I finally decided that I would let them put the tent over my head in order to overcome my fear. As I lay there, I heard, "Do not fear water since you were born in water; you are made up of ninety-five percent water; you need to drink water to survive; water cannot hurt you," etc. We are told to drink a lot of water; it is healthy for our skin, organs, etc. One of the elements for survival around us, besides air, is water. Water became a metaphor, a karmic healing for me, and now a wonderful friend. We need to live in balance with the elements. Is it possible that water comes through the regressions as a reminder that we are off-balance with the elements?

Another theme that pops up is the reliability of our psychicness, our intuitive skills, and our gut feelings. We all have these skills, yet we do not seem to trust them. In fact, our gut or intuition is our truth. We must listen, but our intellect seems to get in the way. We can all develop our intuition if we choose to do so. Practice does make perfect.

We need to learn how to separate the gut from the intellect and choose what is appropriate at the appropriate time. Usually, the gut will be right. However, we have intellect to help us make the right choices. Sometimes even the truth needs to be tempered. Being more psychic or open gives us greater insight into our present life as well as our past lives.

Trusting in the Universal Order of Things

Besides our highest source and the help or protection we are offered by our spiritual guides, one of the most important resources in life is the universal order of things. We must trust and believe that being patient will allow things to happen when they are supposed to. We must trust and find our truth within ourselves, knowing that we still ultimately have freedom of choice here. We are all where we are supposed to be, doing exactly what we are supposed to be doing. When we fight this, we will find no resolve since we cannot fight the universe.

We must always stay open and listen to the guidance that the universe sends us. It comes through meditation, dream, prayer, synchronicities, people's comments, books, etc. If we ask for something from the universe and we get something else in its place then we must listen to and be grateful for what shows up. The universe knows better than we do what it is that we need.

If we trust that the universe is sending exactly what we need then we will never be disappointed. If we expect that, the universe will lead us to what we need to see or do. Trusting the universe is imperative in order to come into balance with one's self. Since your intuition is connected to the universe, this also means trusting your gut or intuition for the same direction.

When we can truly trust in both God and ourselves then we will always know our direction. The negative emotions such as fear, anger, frustration, sadness, loneliness, etc. will no longer be in our lives.

We sometimes have a different time clock than the universe has. We think something should happen at a certain time, but the universal order or time has a different plan. If we think we have done our work and are waiting for the rewards, perhaps there is still work to be done.

Freedom of Choice

Our greatest gift on both this earth plane and the spiritual plane is that of freedom of choice. No matter what our pre-planned destiny, we still have the gift of freedom of choice. We can change our destiny by making certain decisions that alter the original plan. We can choose to learn our lessons or not. We can be with people we need to clear Karma with or not. By making certain decisions, we can change the course of events, even daily.

There is no right or wrong choice. Whatever we choose, it is the right choice simply because we choose it. The choice may generate Karma, but that will be addressed at a later date or perhaps a later lifetime. We even have freedom of choice to change our choices.

We not only have freedom of choice here but also on the spiritual side. On the spiritual side, we can choose what we need to learn, with whom we would like to spend time, if we want to incarnate, and what the lesson is we need to learn. We choose our parents after we decide the proper time to come. We decide what Karma needs to be worked on and with whom. We decide the geological location where we need to be. We do have guidance in making those decisions on the spirit side, which we learn to embrace. Both in the spirit world and the physical world, our choices are limitless and without judgment.

Synchronicities

Carl Jung introduced us to the word and concept of synchronicities. He defined it as a happening that has personal meaning beyond the intended meaning of that event. I call it *non-coincidence*. If we listen, synchronicities are going on all the time. If we listen, they will always guide us to the right place. It acts as that sixth sense of connection. It is a tool that is used often by the universe to lead us or communicate with us.

One synchronicity can lead to another. The trick is to keep following them. For example, someone asks you how they can develop their psychic ability. You tell them you went to a workshop six years ago to learn just that. You remember the instructor's name and tell your friend. You remind her that it was six years ago and do not know if she still does that work. The very next day, you receive an invitation to a workshop called "How to Develop Your Psychic Ability." The instructor happens to be the person you told your friend about. You also could use some insight on the progress of your book, and she would be the one to help shed light on that subject. Since you have not heard from her in six years and just mentioned her to your friend and could use this insight, is it coincidence or synchronicity?

Communication with the Dead

Many psychics have claimed that they have communicated with the dead. So many have given proof of their authenticity by repeating messages from loved ones that only they could have known. Many people have trouble believing the evidence since it would mean that they would have to believe that we really do not die but shed our physical body and go someplace from where we can communicate.

This place is called the astral plane. We go to this place when we first die. We meet with other people with whom we had relationships from the earth plane who have also died. We also meet with spirit guides or masters who teach us what we need to learn. Everything is exactly like on earth, except it is more ethereal. We need not eat, drink, etc., but we can if we need it for our healing.

If we need to communicate with our loved ones on earth, we can do it through psychics, dreams, or communication tools such as angel cards. Those on the other side are usually trying hard to get messages to loved ones on the earth plane. We either do not remember dreams or, if we do, we do not think they were real. If we are not open to receiving messages, we will not hear them. Some receive personal information from the psychics and do not believe them, thinking it is some type of a trick. Researchers have proven psychic ability by using various tests showing different brain waves and patterns when channeling in from the other side. (Read *We Never Die* by George Anderson.)

We also have heard to let the dead rest in peace. If they need to, they will rest in peace, but most of them want to be busy working. Almost all want to reach their loved ones. This form of communication can be of great comfort to both parties.

Meditation

Life is a busy place. It can generate great stress and tension. We need a place to quiet our minds, gain insights, and rebalance with the world and its elements. Mediation can help us heal as it strengthens. Through this process, we can reach our own truths within. We gain clarity, and it teaches us how to ground. This process can also help strengthen our immune systems. Meditation teaches us to be open and to listen.

Respect for All Living Things

The process of doing is more important than reaching our destination. Since we are here to learn lessons, the process is what teaches us those lessons. Everyone is a child of God. We all have God's breath within us.

We all feel, think, eat, drink, and experience emotions. According to the Shamans, we have all been animals, trees, earth, and water. If we have been all of these things then no human's life is more important than even our animals. If this is so, we truly are all equal to all things.

Due to our disrespect for each other and the earth, we are suffering. There are wars, murders, scandals, pollution, and drugs. Due to this disrespect, we are in trouble. We tend to judge each other by our differences, feeling negative thoughts about our differences with each other.

Our intolerance manifests as physical actions or energetic actions, which leads to causing harm to each other. Our greed for material things, from meat to furs, has cost us animal life that is just as precious as our own. If we have been animals in the past, how can we not respect them as we do our human population? Even if we eat animals for survival, can't we minimize this by supplementing other foods?

As we take from the earth, we should replenish so as not to harm our environment by ravaging the land. We need to always ask the animals and lands for forgiveness and give them thanks for feeding us and providing for our own survival.

The Essene community revered the fish. They held fish in the highest regard. They felt that it was the highest act of sacrifice and unconditional love that a living form could offer. The fish agreed to come to this earth plane to offer itself to man as a food source so that man could evolve to a higher level. It asked for nothing in return. The Essenes would bury the fish bones in the burial container in hopes that the next incarnation for the human would evolve as high as the fish. They hoped that they would evolve beyond the human form and come into this life next time with such unconditional love and service as the fish gives to mankind.

Animals certainly have their own evolution, but let us stop to look at their role in society. Have they chosen to come in a lower life form for our evolution? Have they come here to teach us how to live in harmony with all of life? Don't they respect the boundary man and nature have presented? Don't they eat just for survival? We must learn and respect the animal kingdom, for we could not survive without them.

We must also respect the Mother Earth that has nurtured and fed us with her food and water. We must respect and love our fellow man with which we must share the wealth of our earth. Only then can we live the way we have been created, in balance and with awe for life.

Intention

When a client comes in with an issue, illness, relationship problem, or question, I take a history intake to see where there may be any patterns in their life. I listen for red flags that may alert me to an important piece of information that is affecting their issue. We come to an agreement as to the best way to form a verbal intention for the subconscious to look for that memory. While under hypnosis, we will give the subconscious the intention so it can find the memory and regress us back to that time.

Earth Plane

While we are incarnated on this earth, we are on the earth plane. When we leave our bodies, we go to the next plane, called the astral plane. This is where we meet our loved ones, light beings, or angels who help guide us as to what we need to do next.

As we evolve, we keep moving into different planes. Some of us go directly to a more evolved plane if we have been through this process many times and feel we do not need to stop in the astral plane first.

In my experience, most of us have had many lifetimes. I have not had any clients for whom this incarnation was their first. Other colleagues have had some for whom this was their first incarnation, but such a thing seems to be pretty rare.

ADD/ADHD

ADD stands for *attention-deficit disorder* and ADHD is *attention-deficit hyperactive disorder*. The diagnosis tells us that such children or adults cannot focus and are easily distracted. Some are more energetic than others. This population has been over-diagnosed and treated with medication that might have been avoided if they had tried this work first.

I have seen a pattern of individuals with ADD cases who had died in a war in a past life. The current ADD client reports from the past life, "I never saw it coming" due to being distracted and unfocused.

Last Thoughts

The last thought we have before we leave this earth is one of the most important times of our lives. Our next life can be a whole new life drama around that thought or part of one. It could also bring us into the next life with a physical illness, malady, or block around money or relationships. We must try to leave as clear as we can, forgiving others and ourselves. A good question to ask someone before they die is, "If you could have changed anything, what would have done differently?" We need to help them fulfill it using visualization.

Parallel Universe

There are some people who believe that we are living our lives all at the same time—the past, present, and future. That can explain why we can have an overlap of lifetimes when doing regression work. I believe that may be why our soul feels so tired. So much we do not know!

Archetypical Energy

Many times we need to work out some issue that we may not be able to find in one of our past lives. It may hold more significance if we use an archetypical figure or story to work out our issue. Our subconscious will come up with one if we can heal on a deep level using it. For example, if we are going through betrayal issues in this life, we could go back to a lifetime as Simon Peter. We may not have been him, but we know so much about his story that we can use it to clear our own issue.

Messages from Spirit

At the end of every lifetime, I bring my client to another dimension to access their guardian angel, spirit guide, the masters, the light, or their higher self. I direct my client to ask questions to these guides: the client's lessons, purpose, and any other question we may have.

We also ask these guides for any messages they may have for us from loved ones who have passed.

This chapter holds a compilation of messages my clients have received over the years. Some are lessons for our greatest growth and understanding, and some are just messages sent out of love. These messages are universal, and they will leave the reader feeling richer by remembering these truths.

Messages from Guides

How much do we give to others? Always give until it is to your detriment.

You have come into this world to love and be loved.

You are a perfect child of God. Only your life dramas and old tapes make you feel differently.

If life were easy, we wouldn't change. Only when we are in discomfort do we want to change to move out of it.

We are here to learn one dominant lesson, even though we learn many lessons.

We choose to come to the earth plane to learn our lessons versus learning them on spirit side since we learn so much faster in a dense, emotional, and physical body.

There is no judgment if we do not learn our lesson here. There are always opportunities to learn them on spirit side or in our next incarnation.

Healing always starts with an open heart and love.

I almost drowned! Do not fear water. You are made up of seventy-five percent water. You were born in water. You need to drink water to live. The earth is made up of two-thirds water.

Mother Earth really loves you. She feels emotions as well.

We life-script before we come to earth, but we have free will. So we can change the script at any time.

All past lives are not awful! Most of them are wonderful, but we work on those that create issues for us here.

Children can remember well through dreams, play, and cellular memory.

When you can no longer carry the burden then surrender. You do have help.

Messages from Loved Ones

Just think of us, and we will be with you.

Tell my husband I love him, and he needs to eat better.

You were my best friend.

Tell my little girl that I am sorry I had to leave her so young.

Thank God someone is listening. Please tell my wife to be open to receiving. I will have a message for her.

I did not commit suicide; it was an accident that happened so fast.

Do not give up on my boy. Please look after him.

Yes, it is me you feel in the middle of the night stroking your hair.

I heard your whispers while I was lying there in the hospital. Thank you.

I felt you all around my bed just before I passed. Thank you for letting me go.

I just could not do it anymore. I just felt so trapped in the physical body.

We will be together again—always.

You did everything you could. I am so grateful.

You have angels all around you.

I am here with your Uncle Paul and other family.

I have no more pain. I am whole once again.

Watch for signs from me.

I will send you a sign of a butterfly.

Wear the locket you have of mine. It means a lot to me.

You do not have to stay in that house anymore. You can sell it.

Take care of Pogo.

Forget how it ended. I am more peaceful now.

I want my family to live life like a beautiful light.

Thank you for rubbing my feet, for leaving the window open so I could hear the children playing, and for tirelessly talking to me.

I chose to come into this life to leave early so you would learn how to be strong.

I am finally home.

WE ARE WHO WE HAVE BEEN…

WE CAN CHANGE WHO WE ARE AT ANY GIVEN TIME WITH
OUR FREE WILL BY THE
CHOICES WE MAKE.

CHOOSE WISELY, THINK WISELY, SPEAK WISELY — FOR YOU
ARE CREATING YOUR
FUTURE AND THE FUTURE OF THOSE YOU TOUCH.

NOT THE END — ONLY THE BEGINNING

About the Author

In private practice since 1989, Saundra C. Blum is a certified Ericksonian hypnotherapist and Past Life Regression Therapist. Her formal education consists of a master's of science degree in special education and counseling and a bachelor's of science degree in English and education.

Saundra C. Blum is on the advisory board for Western Connecticut State University's Institute for Holistic Health Studies. In 1998, she co-founded the Katonah Study Group for Integrative Medicine with well-known psychiatrist and author Dr. Mark Banschick. Approximately four hundred members have gathered to explore the most current modalities and techniques in integrative medicine, allopathically and holistically, as well as other, more esoteric fields.

From 2007 –2009, Blum was on the board of directors of the International Association for Research and Regression Therapy ("IARRT"), which is her past-life professional organization, and helped put together many conferences in New York, Massachusetts, Connecticut, and Virginia. She is also a group leader for IARRT, holding monthly experiential workshops and trainings in addition to managing her private practice in Katonah, New York. Between her workshops and private practice, Ms. Blum has seen more than four thousand clients over the past twenty-four years.

Ms. Blum has participated in advanced workshops and seminars with top regressionists such as Brian Weiss, Roger Wolger, Edith Fiore, Winifred Lucas, and Joseph Casta. She has lectured to a plethora of colleagues in the mental health field and medical community. She also trains and certifies Past Life Regressionists in northern Westchester County, New York, as well as internationally in mind-body-spirit-centered cultures, such as India and Italy.

Due to her international reputation, Ms. Blum has been sought out to help organize and coordinate a number of conferences and workshops, including two New York IARRT conferences and a conference workshop for the Edgar Casey Institute in Virginia Beach and Sturbridge, Massachusetts. In addition, she has created, organized, and presented a new international integrative medicine model for practitioners in Tuscany, Italy (2010).

Ms. Blum has given a number of media interviews, including on "Fox 5 National News" and local cable station shows such as "Beyond the Realm," based in White Plains, New York. She has been invited to host radio programs by wellness-oriented radio station WEVD, one of the largest health stations on the East Coast, and she was asked to participate in a holistic program on WABC. She has been the subject of articles for such publications as the *Hudson Valley Magazine* as well as local papers, including the *Bedford Record*.

Ms. Blum lives in Westchester County, New York, with her husband, Michael. They have two grown children.

Ms. Blum's second book, *The Gift – Synchronicity through Divine Intervention*, is scheduled to be released in the near future. The book shares a life-changing journey that she and a client took to factually validate the client's past-life experiences from the 1920s.